Living your Best

D.A.S.H.

Are you **D**aring to **A**chieve a **S**uccessful and **H**appy Life?

Author

Patti Stueland

Copyright © 2025 by Patti Stueland

All rights reserved. No part of this publication may be reproduced, distributed or transmitted in any form or by any means, without prior written permission.

Author Patti Stueland / Kez Publishing
Western Australia, Australia

kezwickhamstgeorge.com

Category Non-fiction

Book Layout © 2025 womensbizglobal.com

Living your Best D.A.S.H. / Patti Stueland - 2nd ed.
ISBN 979-8-9913451-0-1

Dedication

I want to dedicate this book to three special people who have and continue to fill my life with Passion and Purpose and have taught me in so many ways what it means to not only live my best life, but to live my best DASH: My mom, Carolyn Stueland, my dad, Bob Stueland and my partner, Whit. You have loved, supported, and taught me the real meaning of Daring to Achieve a Successful and Happy life. I thank you and love and appreciate you all.

ACKNOWLEDGMENT

I would like to take this opportunity to express my heartfelt gratitude to all those who have played a part in making Living Your Best *DASH:* Are you 'Daring to Achieve a Successful and Happy Life' a reality. This book is the culmination of years of reflection, exploration, and personal growth, and it would not have been possible without the unwavering support and encouragement of so many incredible individuals.

First and foremost, I want to extend my deepest appreciation to my family and friends who have stood by me throughout this journey. Your belief in me and constant encouragement have been the driving force behind my pursuit of living my best *DASH.* Thank you for always being there to lift me up and inspire me to reach for the stars.

I would also like to extend my thanks to the countless mentors, coaches, and teachers who have imparted their wisdom and guidance throughout my personal and professional journey. Your knowledge, encouragement, and unwavering belief in my potential have been instrumental in shaping my understanding of passion and purpose. Your generosity in sharing your expertise has truly made a profound impact on my life.

To the readers and supporters of this book, thank you for embarking on this transformative journey with me. Your openness, curiosity, and willingness to explore living your best DASH are an inspiration to me. It is my sincerest hope that this book serves as a guide, igniting the flames of passion within each of you and empowering you to live a purposeful and fulfilling life. And finally, I want to express my deepest gratitude to God, the universe, and all the forces at work that have guided me on this path of self-discovery. Thank you all from the bottom of my heart for being part of this incredible journey. May we continue to support and uplift each other as we explore what it means to be *Daring to Achieve a Successful and Happy life, and create a world filled with love, joy, and fulfillment.*

Life's an Adventure, Enjoy the Journey!

Enjoy your Dash.

Patti

CONTENTS

PROLOGUE 1
GROWING UP 1
WINNERS NEVER QUIT AND QUITTERS NEVER WIN 7
A POSITIVE MENTAL ATTITUDE 11
CHOICES AND CONSEQUENCES 17
DON'T LET OTHER PEOPLE 'YUCK YOUR WOW'S 23
THE DAY THAT CHANGED MY LIFE 29
DECISION TIME 37
A ROAD LESS TRAVELED. MY STORY OF LOST BEARINGS .. 41
NAVIGATING THE ABYSS 49
EMBRACING HELP, A PATH TO HEALING 55
LIFE'S AN ADVENTURE, ENJOY THE JOURNEY 63
MAKE IT A GREAT DAY OR NOT, THE CHOICE IS YOURS ... 69
I'M H-A-P-P-Y 75
HEALTHY 81
APPRECIATE 87
POSITIVE 93
PLAYFUL 99
THE POWER OF YES 105
PRIORITIZING SELF-CARE AND SELF-LOVE 109
LET GO AND LET GOD 115
WHAT DOES D.A.S.H MEAN? 121
DARING 127
ACHIEVE 133
SUCCESSFUL 139

HAPPY	145
YOUR LIFE MATTERS	151
BONUS	157
SPECIAL THANKS	165
ABOUT THE AUTHOR	167

PROLOGUE

Living your best D.A.S.H.

Are you Daring to Achieve a Successful and Happy life?

Hello and welcome to 'Living your best D.A.S.H. Throughout this book, you will learn what it means to be 'Daring to Achieve a Successful and Happy life' I am the Chief Pathfinder of my business Pathways with Patti, and I am truly excited you have chosen to read this book. I look forward to being your tour guide on this journey called *Living Your Best Dash*. As I write, I am listening to the wisdom within this book. In fact, I want you to give yourself a round of applause. While you're at it, pat yourself on the back' for making yourself a priority.

As we all travel on this pathway called life, how many of you can look back upon your life and see all the different trails you have wondered and explored? Go ahead, raise your hand, it's great validation. Did those trails and paths always get you to your expected destination? Or were there a few detours along the way? How many of you have had that experience? Without those detours along the way, you wouldn't be here right now reading this book. There's a reason for that. Our life's roadmap didn't come with the perfect G.P.S. or instruction manual on how to travel through the peaks and valleys of this thing called life. Along the way, we needed to pull off at that rest stop to relax and restore our strength for the next leg of our journey. How many of you have found this to be true? If so, raise your hand.

The goal and main purpose of this book is for you to look at your life up to this point and decide if you are enjoying the journey. If you are happy with what you have done and where you are going, congratulations. Way to go, for those of you still thinking about it, guess what? It's never too late to create a legacy you can be proud of. How cool is that! Sometimes all we need is a little tune up or adjustment to rediscover our passion and purpose. Others of us are looking for a major overhaul. Whichever path you happen to be on currently, you are in the right place at the right time. The best way to discover your path and the direction you choose to follow is to read each chapter in this book. After you finish each chapter, then go to the Journeys Guide and follow the self-discovery questions and activities.

Ok, go ahead and start this new journey.

Learn how to continue or begin to

'Live your best D.A.S.H.'

Life's an Adventure, Enjoy the Journey.

Patti

CHAPTER ONE

GROWING UP

'Laughter is timeless, Imagination has no age, and Dreams are forever.'

by Walt Disney

All of us have a starting point on this pathway called life. I would like to start by sharing with you my 'Pathway of Self Discovery.' I grew up in Southern California in a town called Chino, that in 1965 was a very small town. For me, it was a fantastic town to grow up in. The community looked out for each other and supported each other. Everyone attended the athletic events at Chino High School whether you had children attending the school or not. In kindergarten, I started my Girl Scout journey as a Brownie along with a handful of my friends. For some of you, you can see in your imagination right now what that Brownie uniform looked like can't you? I can see that smile on your face.

My Dad worked for Southern California Edison and the number one statement he would say to us three kids is 'I just work for the Edison Company; I do not own it. Turn off the lights if you're done in that room.' My Mom was a full-time wife and mother to me and my two siblings. The hardest job I know, and she was incredible. The reason I chose the Walt Disney quote at the beginning of this chapter is because of my parents and the village' of loved ones that helped to create the foundation of my life. Laughter, imagination and dreams were all major themes during my childhood. Growing up, my village consisted of both sets of grandparents, aunts, uncles, cousins, family friends, church members, teachers, and friends.

With each group in my village, almost daily there was laughter. You know the saying *'Laughter is the best medicine'*. It's true. And, if it's a belly laugh, that's the best right there. Did you know that laughter according to 'Active beat' is a natural pain killer. It strengthens your heart, wards off disease, tones your stomach muscles, boosts your Immunity, decreases blood pressure, can banishes stress, and last bit not least, helps those suffering from depression. Isn't that amazing? I call this, the Power of Laughter. The effect that laughter has on us is transformative and almost astounding, I have found laughter to be a powerful tool that uplifts, motivates, and inspires us in every aspect of our lives.

When someone was feeling down or not well, the healing power of that laughter provided a type of time-out from the pain and lifted the spirits of everyone around at that Moment. This was one way of how I learned at a very early age that even in challenging times, joy could be found. Laughter is contagious and it can spread like wildfire among us.

I found that when people from my village were together and we laughed together we formed stronger bonds which strengthened that sense of belonging and acceptance of one another. No matter what our differences, laughter always created an inclusive and supportive environment. As E. Cummings said, *'The most wasted of all days is one without laughter.'* My question for you at this point which you will also find in the Journey's Guide, why does it seem as we get older that we tend to get so serious, and laughter takes a backseat? It seems to me that as we age, laughter needs to be in the front seat of our life. Especially when you know all the amazing physical, mental and spiritual benefits of laughter. As a kid, I'm not even sure I knew what the word imagination meant until I watched Walt Disney every Sunday night on our TV, introducing that week's episode of World of Disney before setting up that week's show. Walt would tell us about what was happening with the expansion of Disneyland, building Walt Disney World and what the Imagineers were creating.

By seeing the maps of those plans and Walt telling us what his vision was for each amusement park I didn't realize then at five years old that he was teaching me what was possible when you use your imagination. Playing with my friends and creating forts and castles made from blankets and sheets given to us by my mom, we created an entire imaginary world and characters. Believing for that moment in time that was our reality. On rainy days, my mom would set up a little table and chairs for my siblings on our exceedingly small front porch and set out magazines and newspapers. She would mix flour and water making it into a paste. She would then give us each a piece of paper, scissors, and popsicle sticks. I was so excited to share my masterpiece with my mom and dad. The idea was to cut out things from magazines and newspapers and create something on our piece of paper, using our imaginations. I would lie in the grass in our front yard as a kid and look up at the sky and imagine what the shapes of the clouds looked like to me and totally fascinated by it all.

Little did I know that when I started kindergarten and I met my teacher, Mrs. Gasman, that she would be the one who put into motion what my future career would be. From her style of teaching, she encouraged us to use our imaginations and dream of the possibilities in everything we did. Although I didn't really know or understand that at the time. I just knew because of her teaching us this superpower, teaching was what I wanted to do when I grew up. I wanted to be a kindergarten teacher. From that moment on, no matter the grade I was in, I knew I was going to be a teacher, only the subject and age group that I would teach changed. Just as Walt Disney mentioned in the opening quote, imagination has no age.' Even now in my sixties, I imagine the possibilities of what my life can be, where I can go, what I can do. Can you remember using your imagination when you were younger? How about now? Part of living your best life is imagining all the possibilities of what can be.

The final part of Walt Disney's quote says, 'Dreams are forever.' Did you ever pick a dandelion, make a wish, and blow on it and watch as each of those feathery seeds of the dandelion launched into the air? Or make a wish as you blew out the candles on your birthday cake, tossed a coin in a fountain and made a wish? All of these are a part of dreaming. Dreaming doesn't happen only when you are sleeping. In the Disneyland song 'Wish upon a Star,' it says; 'when you wish upon a star, your dreams come true.' Those wishes and dreams can come true if you believe. Remember a time when you were growing up and anything and everything was possible? That sense of wonder, dreaming of a future that was exciting, and met our every need and desire. Never stop dreaming and believing in what you can achieve in your life.

Journey's Guide

In your favorite-colored pen, write down three (3) things that brought you joy during your childhood.

1.

2.

3.

In a different colored pen, write about what you wanted to be when you grew up. Was it just one thing or several occupations? Did you become what you wanted? Why or why not? Before closing out this chapter, close your eyes, take a couple of deep breaths, think about the things you just wrote about. Remember what brought you happiness and joy as a child. Feel that smile form as you reminisce about the joyful times. Bring to the forefront of your mind that you are never too old to dream and imagine the life you desire and deserve.

CHAPTER TWO

WINNERS NEVER QUIT AND QUITTERS NEVER WIN

'In life, winning and losing will both happen.
What is never acceptable is quitting.'
by Magic Johnson

When I was in the fifth grade, I decided I wanted to play an instrument. I really wanted to play the trumpet, however, that wasn't a choice the after-school music teacher gave me. I could play the flute or the clarinet. The flute looked like it would be too difficult to play, so I chose the clarinet. My parents didn't have much money, so they decided to rent a clarinet to make sure I enjoyed it before buying it. That was a great decision. After a couple of months, I discovered that I really didn't enjoy playing the clarinet at all. I remember coming home from school one day and telling my parents I wanted to stop playing. This is when I learned one of the most valuable life lessons ever when I heard my dad say the following words 'Once you start something, you must finish it. Once it is over and you never want to do it again, you don't have to. By quitting, you are letting your teacher and friends down and most of all, you are not a quitter. So, I played the clarinet the rest of my fifth-grade year and when the school year was over, so was my clarinet career.

Because of that experience, I knew exactly what the expectations for the rest of my life would be. Before I ever began anything, I would think long and hard on whether I really wanted to try out for something or begin something new. During the rest of my public-school years, I saw many other students quit our athletic teams in the middle of the season. It made it more difficult for our team to readjust to that person's decision. Which was always upsetting to the coach and my teammates and myself. These events would only reinforce for me that quitting wasn't an option. Now, I would like to clarify whether someone did quit due to medical reasons or they had to move away, or any other critical matter, that is something entirely different.

Many times, we find ourselves overwhelmed by starting something new or different and it is natural for our brain to tell us to run. It's in those moments that we learn what we are truly made of. I know from personal experience; it was in those moments that I learned the most about myself and learned lessons that have carried me through my life and benefited me in numerous ways.

One year I coached a Junior Varsity high school girls' basketball team. I coached numerous tennis, basketball and softball teams and I had never had what most refer to as a losing season until this particular year. That basketball season we did not win one game. Yep, that's right.

Our season record was 0-14 and here is the amazing part, not one girl quit the entire season. I knew from the beginning of try outs that year, it was going to be a rough season. With that in mind, I changed my coaching strategy and attitude. For every game, we set team goals on what we wanted to accomplish. At the end of each game, we would go over the goals that were set and see how we did. Every single game that season, the girls accomplished the goals. We would celebrate and the girls were excited about their achievements. I reinforced that they were each winner for reaching those goals and because of the atmosphere we created together, our wins came in a different form. When I taught my athletes and students that famous Vince Lombardi quote;

'Winners never quit, and quitters never win' I was also teaching them about perseverance and determination. They may seem to be simple words; however, they are words that convey a universal truth that applies to almost every area of our lives. When we are successful, it is due to our resilience, tenacity, and our commitment to our goals. People who emerge as winners in life are the ones who refuse to be brought down by life's challenges and setbacks.

They are the ones who see obstacles not as roadblocks, but as steppingstones to greater achievements. The path to success is filled with difficulties, but it is the unwavering spirit of a winner that propels them forward. For those that choose to be quitters, they are denying themselves the opportunity to know what it means to taste the sweet fruits of victory. They abandon their aspirations at the first sign of trouble and miss out on the valuable lessons and personal growth that comes from overcoming challenges. Quitting can become a self-imposed limitation, which prevents an individual from realizing their full potential. Whether in academics, sports, career pursuits, or personal development, the philosophy of not quitting serves as a guiding principle. It's what creates resilience, it also creates a strong work ethic, and it instills the belief that with determination, at times even the biggest obstacles can be conquered.

When it comes to living your best Dash, winners are the ones who refuse to be defined by setbacks and prove that perseverance is the key to unlocking success. You are that winner, which doesn't mean that you necessarily score the most points every time or have the best house or highest paying job and the list could go on and on. It means that you deserve the best of what life can offer you whatever that means to you. When you are doing the things that you are enthusiastic about and you know are part of your purpose, even in those tough times, don't quit. Believe you can, and you will, remember you are the winner.

Journey's Guide

1. When you read the quote: 'Winners never quit, quitters never win,' what does that mean to you?

2. How do you believe perseverance and resilience contribute to success?

3. What are some examples of individuals or situations where persistence led to victory?

4. Write down a personal experience where persistence plays a critical role in achieving one of your goals.

CHAPTER THREE

A POSITIVE MENTAL ATTITUDE

'Your mental attitude is something you can control outright, and you must use self-discipline until you create a Positive Mental Attitude. Your mental attitude attracts to you everything that makes you what you are.'

By Napolean Hill

I didn't realize as I was growing up that my parents were laying down a foundation that included Positive Mental Attitude. I was extremely fortunate that the bumps on life's road that my parents experienced from growing up, were used to teach their children to look at life in a way that created something positive out of life's challenges and obstacles. That P.M.A. foundation grew exponentially when I made the varsity softball team in high school. My softball coach was the one who put a name to what my parents had begun with me as a child, and she took it to a whole new level. Everything we did whether it was practice, games, or the social events we did together, our coach's philosophy was to turn that frown upside down, stop that stinkin' thinkin and we never lose, we have temporary setbacks. Goal setting for our team and individually was a priority.

Visualization became another part of our goal setting experience, and I really learned to, 'Dream it, Believe it, Achieve it. This is not to say that a positive mental attitude means that everything will be perfect in your life. What it means is, when the tough times happen and they will and they do, or when we do not make such wise choices for our life, look for ways to take that tough situation or consequence from our choice. Learn the lesson and look for ways to not repeat it, making the next time better. Look for the possibilities. I have shared on several occasions that my life's motto is: 'Life's an Adventure, Enjoy the Journey.' Life's journey is not just about reaching the destination; it's about savoring the Moments along the way. Embrace the highs and lows, the challenges, and victories. Each experience, whether positive or negative, contributes to your growth and shapes who you become. Learn from the harsh times, appreciate the good times, and keep moving forward. Our thoughts have a profound impact on our reality. Cultivate a positive mindset, and you'll attract positivity into your life. When faced with difficulties, focus on solutions rather than dwelling on problems. Replace self-doubt with self-belief and replace fear with courage.

Affirmations can be powerful tools to reinforce positive thinking, so start your day with empowering statements that align with your goals and aspirations. Look at positive mental attitude as being the key to a fulfilling life. A positive mental attitude is also a powerful force that shapes our view of the world. There have been many times over the past ten years where I have needed to take a sabbatical from watching the news on television and even news related shows. As of this moment in time, I have rarely seen the news in the past two years. This isn't to say that I am practicing being an Ostrich with my head stuck in the sand. What it means for me is not taking in all the negative energy that is coming at us from television and social media. Instead of taking in all that negative energy and feeling helpless and hopeless about how I am unable to fix the world's problems, I chose to put my energy into what is happening in my part of the world. I do have control over those things. With a positive mental attitude, I can make a better choice with my responses when it comes to life's challenges. It is not merely a fleeting emotion, but a mindset that significantly impacts my overall well-being and success in life. By embracing a positive mental attitude, it cultivates optimism, resilience, and an initiative taking approach to life's ups and downs.

One of the primary benefits of maintaining a positive mental attitude is its impact on our mental health. Optimistic individuals tend to experience lower levels of stress and anxiety, bringing about better emotional well-being. They approach setbacks as temporary obstacles rather than insurmountable barriers, allowing them to bounce back from adversity more effectively. Research has also shown that a positive outlook can also enhance physical health by boosting our immune system and reducing the risk of chronic illnesses.

A positive mental attitude can also be a driving force behind personal and professional success. People with a positive mindset are more likely to set and achieve goals, as they approach challenges with a can-do attitude. This optimism not only fuels motivation but also brings about positive opportunities and relationships. An important piece I don't want to ignore about P.M.A; it isn't about being positive all the time. Life happens. According to Alexa Brand in her The Positive Thinking Workbook, this is what positive thinking isn't: 'Positive thinking is not viewing everything in a positive light or pretending everything is okay when it's not. That would be toxic positivity. Toxic positivity is the assumption that we must maintain 'positive vibes' even in times of great suffering. It assumes you should ignore your suffering, which is a harmful practice.

When you ignore your suffering, you are not allowing yourself to process our emotions, and they become buried inside of you. This only intensifies your suffering. Additionally, there is no such thing as being perfect at positive thinking. We are human. And finally, positive thinking is not selfish. When you're able to focus on your own well-being, you become better set up to help others in more abundant ways. As the adage goes, 'You can't pour from an empty cup.' On a wall in my classroom was a quote by Dennis Mannering: 'Attitudes are contagious, is yours worth catching?' Every day I would see that quote and was reminded that before my students entered my room, what type of attitude did I want them to 'catch.' That thinking also spread to every area of my life.

I will admit right here and right now, it is not always easy to have a cheerful outlook. Cultivating a positive mental attitude involves intentional efforts to change negative thought patterns and focus on the silver linings. Practice daily writing in a gratitude journal, do mindfulness / meditation exercises, say positive affirmations to help reinforce a positive mindset. When you know better, you do better, and those low times don't last as long, and it is easy to get back to that can-do attitude. It is also imperative to surround yourself with supportive and optimistic people. They can contribute to the development and maintenance of a positive mental attitude. When you embrace positivity, you can unlock your full potential to create a fulfilling and meaningful life. How cool is that!

Journey's Guide

One put down deserves two put ups. Sadly, it is easy to say something negative to someone before you think of something positive to say. I taught my nieces and nephews and my students that when someone 'puts you down' (says something negative to you or about you) tell them they owe you 'two put ups' (two positive statements) Examples: I really like your smile, you are a great athlete, you tell good jokes, etc. Take a few moments to think about someone in your life that tends to be negative towards you. The next time they make a negative remark, tell them 'You owe me two put ups' Be patient and be willing for them to respond with two positive things about you. Break that negative chain.

Below, write down three things that are positive about you.

1.

2.

3.

What are three areas in your life that you would like to focus on being more positive?

1.

2.

3.

CHAPTER FOUR

CHOICES AND CONSEQUENCES

*'In every single thing you do, you are choosing a direction.
Your life is a product of choices.'*

By Dr. Kathleen Hall

As I mentioned in the previous chapter, we don't always make the best choices and decisions in life. Every choice we make, there is a consequence. That consequence can be positive or negative. That choice can make us stronger or sadly for some, it can destroy them. Another area that my parents did a fantastic job of doing was demonstrating to us the importance of choosing wisely when it came to friends. I learned early on that those friendships created bonds that helped me during those challenging times. That is still true for me to this day. When it seemed that the direction that my life was going was going wasn't very productive, I always was able to turn to one of those trusted friends and basically spill my guts. I wasn't always looking for advice. Most of the time, I just needed to let it all out and many times, I discovered on my own what I needed to do or just felt better that someone else knew and cared.

Those same choices we make also put our life on a specific life path. When I look back over my life and see the choices I made, I can almost see a 'road map' that was created to bring me to this very point of my life. If it weren't for those specific choices I made, I wouldn't have had the life experiences I had or met the people who have become family and learned those valuable life lessons for me. Now, that isn't to say that if I had the chance to change a few things, that I wouldn't do them differently. I'm not a person who lives with regrets.

For me to live my 'best dash,' I don't want to come to the end of my life saying, 'I should have, I would have, or I could have.' I want to know if I took advantage of the opportunities that came my way. I want to take advantage of creating a path for my life that has yet to be explored. Knowing from the age of six that I wanted to be a teacher, I knew early on I would need to go to college to make that happen. Up to that point, no female in my family had ever gone to college. Most of the women in my family after high school, got married and started their families. I knew that wasn't the path I wanted for my life. I made choices that put me on that path. I made the choice to make connections with my teachers and coaches and ask them questions. I took advantage of all they would offer me when it came to the courses to take, the paperwork to fill out, the people to meet.

Now, this isn't to say that I made all the right choices or continue to make the right choices. There have been plenty of consequences along my life's journey. What I learned from an early age from my parents was to learn from those consequences, take that knowledge, grow from it, and use that new found knowledge and move forward. This isn't as simple as it sounds. Many times, learning the lesson didn't come overnight or within a week or two. It also doesn't mean that I didn't find myself having a pity party. Having this sort of party is part of the learning and growing we need to do to learn the lesson. Where the problem begins is when we 'pitch a tent' and stay there feeling sorry for ourselves. That's when we need to reach out and find a trusted friend, family member or a professional to help us out. There is nothing to feel bad or embarrassed about needing and/or wanting help. I know for myself, when I get into those dark or frustrating places in my life, I just find my trusted 'person' and talk to them and 'let it out.' It seems to fall into place for me in the following ways.

1. I feel better expressing the frustration or problem.

2. Once I have expressed it, I have more clarity to a possible solution.

3. I have learned many times that I'm not the 'only one' who has had that problem or situation. I am then able to move on and move forward.

Choices and consequences are part of the fabric of our lives. They are part of what shapes and molds our present and our future. Every decision we make, no matter how trivial it may seem, carries the weight of potential outcomes. The path we find ourselves on is the result of the choices we embrace or discard along the way. Whether we are selecting a career path, forming relationships, or deciding on our daily actions, each choice sets off a chain reaction of consequences. These consequences become the ripples that touch not only our lives, but also the lives of those around us.

Keep in mind that there is great power in the choices we make. It defines our character and influences our future. The choices we make can either determine whether we reach our goals or encounter adversity. While some consequences may be immediate and tangible, others may unfold gradually, revealing their impact over time. It is crucial for us to recognize that responsibility accompanies every choice we make.

Becoming aware of the potential consequences challenges us to make thoughtful decisions, considering not only our desires, but also the bigger picture and the implications that go along with it. This journey we navigate is called life and how we make choices and the consequences that come about from those choices is ultimately teaching us about learning, evolving, and shaping our destiny with each step we take. Our lives are 'a product of choices.' Take the time you need to choose wisely.

Journey's Guide

I'd like the following questions to serve as a starting point for you to reflect on the connection between choices and their consequences.

1. Can you provide an example from your own life where you made a choice and experienced both positive and negative consequences?

2. How do personal values influence the choices you make, and what consequences may arise from aligning or conflicting with those values?

3. Reflect on a time when your decision was based on peer pressure. What were the consequences, and what did you learn from that experience?

4. Explore the concept of ethical decision-making. How do your choices align with your ethical beliefs, and what are the potential consequences of compromising those principles?

5. Take a moment to think about the link between goal setting and decision-making. How can setting clear goals help guide your choices, and what happens when choices deviate from those goals?

6. Every day we are influenced by external factors, such as societal norms, cultural expectations, or media, on the choices individuals make. What consequences can arise from blindly following external influences?

7. Reflect on the importance of learning from mistakes. Write down an experience where you made a choice that resulted in negative consequences and the lessons you gained from that situation.

8. Now, take a moment to reflect on a choice you made that resulted in a positive outcome. What were the steps you took in making that choice?

9. With a colored pen, pencil, or marker, use a color that isn't your favorite. Draw a symbol or design on what a negative consequence would look like for you.

10. Using your favorite color pen, pencil, or marker, draw a symbol or design on what a positive choice would look like for you.

CHAPTER FIVE

DON'T LET OTHER PEOPLE 'YUCK YOUR WOWS

'Let Go of people who dull your shine. Poison your spirit. And bring you drama. Cancel your subscription to their issues.'

By Steve Maraboli

Part of my life's mission is to uplift, motivate, inspire, and spread positivity to help people embrace the wonders on this path called life. As we are all aware, this world is filled with challenges and people who want to tear us and others down. My goal in this chapter is to help you find joy in the simplest things that can make a difference. At this point, you may be wondering what I mean by 'Don't Yuck my Wow.'

When we share with others something that is exciting to us, and that person begins to give you a list of reasons why that won't work or basically telling you 'That's a stupid idea.' That person is 'Yucking your Wow' They are not supporting you and they are spreading their negativity onto you and what is important to you. I want to encourage you, the next time that happens to you, reply in this way to that person. 'Don't yuck my Wow.' Many times, that person may not even realize that they are being negative towards your ideas. By making that statement, you stop the

negativity immediately. If they don't understand what you mean by that statement, basically explain to them, if you can't say something nice, don't say anything at all.'
Let us now focus on the Wow and how we can begin 'Embracing the Wow Moments.' Life is a remarkable journey, and every day is an opportunity to discover the extraordinary in the ordinary. Let's celebrate those wow moments that bring a smile to our faces and joy to our hearts. Whether it's watching a beautiful sunset, enjoying a delicious meal, or sharing laughter with loved ones, these little wonders add color to our lives.

So, I'd like you to stop reading this chapter for a moment. Yes, that's what I said, stop reading for just a moment to think about the little wonders that add color to your life. What are the things that bring a smile to your face and fill your heart and soul with joy? Do you even take the time to embrace your wow moments? It's all about taking care of you, your self-love and self-care. You deserve it. When you take time to embrace your wows, you change the direction of your day and the path you are following.

You make yourself a priority in that Moment. It's ok to do that. Once you embrace that Moment, then you are ready to give to others. You will also find it is easier to tell those naysayers to Don't Yuck My Wow. Here are some of my favorite wow nuggets of wisdom with these following quotes. It is my hope that they will resonate deep within to remind you of your limitless potential and encourage you to keep pushing forward on your journey towards greatness. 'Strong People Don't Put Others Down, They Lift Them Up by Motivational Gym Quotes by Zig Ziglar. 'Don't let anyone's ignorance, hate, drama, or negativity stop you from being the best person that you can be. That's rule one.

'Hurt people, hurt people. That's how pain patterns get passed on, generation after generation after generation. Break the chain today. Meet anger with sympathy, contempt with compassion and cruelty with kindness. Greet grimaces with smiles. Forgive and forget about finding fault. Love is the weapon of the future.'
Yehuda Berg

'To lead the people, walk behind them.' Lao Tzu

'I speak to everyone in the same way, whether he is the garbage man or the President of the University.' Albert Einstein

'Never look down on anybody unless you are helping them up.' Jesse Jackson.

In each of these wise quotes, it is a statement that can give us hope and purpose. It is my goal that they urge you to reach higher, embrace challenges and that it will nurture your spirit. As we reach those bumps on this path called life, remember that through the tough times is when we can grow and gain strength from the experience. Embrace positivity, for it's the key to unlocking doors within.

Ralph Waldo Emerson once said.

*'What lies behind us and what lies before us
are tiny matters
compared to what lies within us.'*

Let these words echo in your heart, igniting resilience and joy. Harness your potential and let wisdom guide you to a life of fulfillment and boundless success.'

Remember as well, just as you don't want someone to yuck your wow when someone shares their wow moment with you, think before you respond. A lesson I would do with my leadership students was to give them each a small tube of toothpaste. I wanted them to squeeze out every bit of the toothpaste onto a plate. Once they completed that part of the task, I gave each of them a toothpick and asked them to put every bit of that toothpaste back into the tube using only the toothpick. They learned very quickly it was basically impossible to accomplish the task. The message behind the lesson, once your words leave your mouth, you can never take them back. Words are powerful. They can be used for good or evil. You get to choose how your words affect others. You also get to choose the words you accept from others. I know for many, when someone shares a wow with us, and we have our doubts about the thoughts and ideas of that person's 'wow,' we really believe we are being helpful with our response.

Take just a moment to think of the best way of wording your response. Think how you want others to respond to you when you share your good news or great ideas. To go one step further with the 'toothpaste' lesson, I asked my students to respond in the following way when they felt someone was yucking their wow. 'You owe me two put ups.' To expand just a bit on that statement: the next time 'you just put me down and you owe me two put ups.' That person needs to say two pleasant things about you. Many times, that person may not even realize this is what they have done. Sadly, there are those who know exactly what they are saying to 'put you down.' Take a stand for yourself and ask them to give you two put ups. Watch what happens when you make that statement.

I taught this lesson to my students and my nieces and nephews and believe me when I tell you, they took this lesson to heart and were more than happy to call me out when I unknowingly put them down. It would stop me in my tracks. It would then create for me a mental note to think briefly before I speak. It really does have an influence on both the person who has been put down and the person speaking the negative talk. Try it, I believe you will like it. Now, go out there, start your day or continue your day, be in the moment. Remember to embrace the wow moments by taking that walk on the beach, registering to go back to school, book that trip, sign up for that art class, begin writing that book, enjoy that cup of tea. Celebrate the wows and joys of life. Also, know when to 'zip your lip'. May these 'words of wisdom' inspire you to inspire and uplift others.

Journey's Guide

1. What does Don't yuck my Wow mean to you? What example(s) can you write about where this saying might be applicable?

2. Think of a time when someone yucked your wow. How did it make you feel, and how did you manage it? On the flip side, have you ever been the person who unintentionally diminished someone else's excitement or accomplishment? How could you have managed that situation differently?

3. Time for some creativity. Design a visual representation that illustrates the concept of 'Don't yuck my wow.' Include key elements that show the essence of the quote and its potential impact on relationships and communication. Share this with a trusted person.

4. Keep the creativity flowing with writing a short story, essay or poem that is inspired by 'Don't yuck my wow.' I would love for you to share this by emailing me a copy of what you have written.

CHAPTER SIX

THE DAY THAT CHANGED MY LIFE

Welcome to chapter six, by now, some of you may be thinking; Patti sure sees life through rose-colored glasses and nothing gets her off track or gets her down. Over the next couple of chapters, I would like to share with you a couple of the big events that happened to me and basically changed my life. This event took place when I was thirty-five years old. Up to this point in my life, this was the most horrific thing to ever happen to me. Since becoming a motivational speaker, this event has become one of my signature talks I have done when speaking to kids and adults.

Welcome The Day That Changed My Life.

It was a beautiful July morning! My motorhome had been fully inspected by a local mechanic and after having $800 dollars of repairs done, I would be ready to hit the road after I packed all camping essentials. My partner Whit and I were heading to Shaver Lake in the Sierra's to meet up and camp with my family. In all the previous years of going on this trip, our family had all caravanned together to get to Shaver Lake. However, this year I had some school business to attend and was unable to leave a few days earlier with the family. Early on a Sunday morning, Whit and I headed to the City of Laverne to pick up Melinda, a 9-year-old friend of my nieces who also happened to be the daughter of my principal. We arrived safely in Laverne and collected Melinda's camping items and are once again ready to go rock-n-roll. However, when I tried to start the motor home, *nothing!* What to do? Looking back now, I see that this was God's first attempt at telling me not to go on! My principal sets up her car so we can jump the battery to see if the motorhome will start and hallelujah it does!! *On The Road Again!* Nothing is going to stop me! I'm going on vacation in the Sierra's.

Now, you need to know something before going any further with my story. This happened in the days before cell phones were around. As you hear more of my story, this little bit of information will help you to see how this modern-day convenience could have changed many things that are about to happen during this one day. It is now 7 am and we are back on the road. After we had driven for about an hour, there was a huge Loud Boom. I look at my passenger side mirror and see black strips of rubber showering out the back of the motorhome and quickly pull over to the emergency lane. Sure enough, one of the inside back tires has popped.

Now, as a teenager, my dad did his fatherly duty by teaching his daughter how to change the tire. However, there was no way I would be able to get the outside tire off and then get to the inside tire to replace it with my spare tire. Again, looking back, this is now God's second attempt to tell me not to go on this trip, did I listen? No, I was determined I was going camping in the Sierra's. Lucky for us, we see a billboard showing at the next offramp is "Juan's Tire Service". The RV hobbles down the freeway to the next exit and we find Juan's place. As if it hasn't already been an eventful morning, Juan does not speak any English and none of us speaks any Spanish. Thank goodness for pantomime and sign language! I point out to Juan the destroyed tire and then show him the spare. Juan nods and goes to work. After 30 minutes and $50 later, we are *on the road again*. Because we are going to the Sierra's!

As we approach Fresno, it is now 10 am and once again we hear Boom, are you kidding me? I once again pulled over and saw that the spare that Juan put on for us had popped. So here we are on a Sunday morning in Fresno, looking for an open tire dealership. We discovered a Goodyear tire shop; however, they don't carry any tires for motorhomes. The shop worker recommends trying the Firestone store which is a couple of miles down the road. To this point in this adventure, have I been listening to God? No. And I am not listening to his third warning not to continue this trip, no, I'm going camping in the Sierras.

The Firestone shop had four RV tires, so I told our very helpful dealer to find the four worse tires on the RV and replace them all! Four hundred dollars and almost two hours later we have four brand new tires on the motorhome, and we are *on the road again.* Because we are going to the Sierra's. I had told my parents before they had left for Shaver Lake that I would be there on Sunday at noon. They knew I was always on time, but here it is 1pm in the afternoon, and we are in Fresno with at least another hour and a half to go before reaching the campground. Remember earlier I mentioned this is before cell phones. I know that my family will give me 30 minutes after my expected arrival time due to possible traffic, stopping at the Purple Plum fruit stand or any other unforeseen circumstances. So not only am I worried about being late, I know shortly they will also be worried.

Before leaving Fresno, I decided to fill up the gas tank, so I won't have to pay those terribly high mountain gas prices. One hundred dollars of gas later, we are *on the road again* Because we are going to the Sierra's. As we began to leave Fresno, it is now 110 degrees, and the motorhome is like a sauna inside. So, I turn on the generator to run the RV air-conditioner. This is so I won't have to use the air that runs off the engine. We are getting ready to move up to an elevation of 5600 feet and I certainly don't want the air conditioner to heat up the engine and then we would have engine problems, heaven forbid. We finally begin our accent into the Sierra's, yay. We passed a motorhome on the side of the road that overheated, and I feel sorry for that couple. Not a fun thing to happen. Later, I would wish that was the only thing that had happened to us.

Whenever I am driving my RV, I am good at pulling over if I am on a two-lane highway so faster drivers can pass. If I see that I have a driver(s) behind me, I look for the next turnout and pull over. I am now about 20 minutes from reaching my destination, Shaver Lake. *Strike up the Band.* Suddenly, I see in my side view mirror a car behind me, flashing its lights and honking his horn at me, I am sure he wants to pass me, however, there is no place for me to pull over. Before I knew it, I saw him crossing over the double yellow lines, driving up alongside of me in the opposite lane of traffic still flashing his lights and honking his horn. I am thinking 'Wow' this guy is ticked off and in a hurry.

As his car becomes even with the RV, his passenger side window rolls down, I am expecting foul language to come my way. However, it wasn't swearing words, he was yelling at me. That is not what came out of his mouth, in fact I had to have him repeat what he just said to me; "I *said your motorhome is on fire'* What? I quickly look at my passenger side mirror and see bright red, yellow and orange flames licking out from the back of my motorhome. The gentleman who told me about the fire quickly passes me, and continues on his way. Immediately I pulled over next to a little forest embankment area. Whit and Melinda open the side door and run to the top of the embankment. I grabbed the fire extinguisher and ran to the back of the RV. Quickly I pulled the pin on the extinguisher and squeezed the handle to see the foam begin to extinguish the fire. Hooray, my heart and soul begin to soar with happiness, only to deflate instantly as the foam finishes in the small extinguisher and the bright flames begin to come back with a furry. Immediately another man comes up to me with his fire extinguisher, just like mine and hands it over to me. Again, I pull the pin, squeeze the handle and watch the flames begin to disappear. No, the foam was gone the flames persisted. Sadness crept all over my body.

Another person ran up to me and said, 'to go back in the RV and turn off the engine'. The reason being it would no longer feed the generator and stop the gas from leaving the gas tank where the fire happened to be located. Not even thinking that the RV could explode, I ran inside, turned off the engine, took out the keys, grabbed my wallet and out the door I go, hoping this will defeat this awful fire. Sad to say once again, it was not meant to be, the fire once again came back with a vengeance and began to engulf the entire back half of my motorhome. I stood the same forest embankment with Whit and Melinda telling myself; "It's only a bad dream". By this time, several good Samaritans have stopped traffic and I notice in the distance the arrival of a Highway Patrol officer. Shortly after his arrival, the Forestry Service comes to our rescue. They quickly jump from the truck, extend the fire hose and the flames recede once again! But luck was not on our side as we began to watch and listen to the tires begin to explode one by one, causing the forestry workers to back away from the half-burned RV rubble. Shortly after the tires finished exploding, the loudest explosion of all occurred, the gas tank. It is here I must tell you that I have parked the RV on a 6 % grade on this mountain road. So, as the full tank of gasoline explodes the flaming liquid begins to run down along the side of the road and begins to start the forest on fire.

I hear God in my sub-conscious saying; "I warned you three times not to take this trip, did you listen, no! You were determined to go camping in the Sierra's." The Captain of the Forestry Service runs up to me and tells me his crew has to stop working on the RV fire due to the forest fire becoming their number one priority. He is very apologetic and looks so sad to not be able to help us any longer. What else is there for us to do? We stand on that forest embankment and watch the remaining sections of the RV burn to the ground. As we stand there in total disbelief, we begin to realize we only have what we are wearing, everything else is gone.

As soon as the fire has burned itself out, the highway patrol officer approaches us to see if we want to see if anything is salvageable. Somehow my brain triggers my voice to respond and say 'sure'. There were actually three items we were able to rescue: 1. Whit's school keys 2. My Dutch oven and 3. A single domino. We knew there was nothing else that had survived this vicious fire, the patrolman asked us to have a seat in the back of his patrol car to relax for a few minutes. He then tells me that he will take us to our campground as soon as the tow truck arrives. As soon as he talks about a tow truck coming, I stare dumbfounded by what they think is towable. There is nothing but a skeleton frame of what was once my motorhome, nothing else is left. There is no more *on the road* again for this RV.

The officer asked if we would like him to take a picture of the RV for insurance purposes and I told him I would really appreciate that. Right then my inner voice told me to have us in the picture with the burnt remains. Adding a little levity to the situation. Let's turn this big burnt lemon into the sweetest tasting lemonade, so the three of us grab the surviving Dutch oven, Whit's school keys and the lone surviving domino and stand alongside the ashes of my once beautiful motorhome. Let's take this picture. The officer takes out his Polaroid camera and clicks the button. The picture has been taken, then the three of us climb into the patrol car's back seat thinking I can begin to relax with relief, this horrible nightmare is finally over.

While the three of us are sitting in the patrol car, Melinda begins to cry, I put my arm around her and told her everything would be alright. With tears streaming down her face, she says to me, "you don't understand, my mom bought me a new Winnie the Pooh sweatshirt and gave me $20, and it's gone" I was momentarily dumbstruck by her statement as I was thinking of the more than $30,000 worth of *things* that were just destroyed. Then I realized that to this sweet young child, how important her things meant to her, my response was "I will buy you another Winnie the Pooh sweatshirt and give you $20", she seemed to be happy with that response. At this point, what else could happen? We were good to go, well, that was another mistake in my thinking. Little did I know that a gentleman who saw the motorhome burning would end up at the local gas station, and they just happened to know my brother. My brother was filling his car with gas and my dad came along for the ride. This friend of my brother says, 'Hey Stu, did you happen to see that motorhome on fire down the road?" My dad and brother knew instantly it was my motor home, because I was now four hours late!

They immediately get into Stu's car and rush to the scene, upon arriving, they don't see Whit, Melinda, or me. All they see is a road full of ashes with a front bumper with an attached license plate showing. Why do I mention the license plate? Several years earlier, I had bought this RV from my parents who were buying a newer RV, so my dad knew exactly what the license plate number was on this motorhome. I also need to tell you before going any further that my dad had heart issues. Now that my dad knows that pile of ash is indeed my RV. He doesn't see any of us, he believes we have died, and he collapses to the ground. My brother calls out to the forestry service guys to see if any of them can help my dad, gratefully a couple of them go over to assist.

CHAPTER SEVEN

DECISION TIME

In the meantime, as we were sitting in the back of the patrol car, I had seen my brother and dad pull up to the scene. Immediately I am thrilled to see them and bewildered as to how they knew to come here. I tried to open the door, and it would not open. Whether it was due to forgetting or just not realizing that the back doors on any law enforcement vehicle do not open so the not so nice cannot escape. It is then that I witness my dad collapsing to the ground and I know he thinks we're dead. I began to claw and bang on the door to get the patrol officer's attention; he hears my banging and runs over to my door to open it. Quickly, I exited the car and ran over to my dad where he is now conscience and hooked up to oxygen. The first words from my lips are, 'dad we are alive, I'm okay, all of us are fine.' He looks up at me and begins to cry, once we know that my dad is good to go, we pile into my brother's car and travel to Shaver Lake Campground. We finally made it, not the way I expected, but we are here.

As my brother pulls into the camping spot that was intended for my RV, my mom, sister-in-law, plus my two young nieces and nephew stare at his car dumbfounded asking where is the RV? We slowly exit his car, and I begin the tale of this horrendous day. After telling our story, my parents began to put together a type of care package for us, items like toothpaste, hairbrushes and clothes to sleep in.

The next day, we have a decision to make. Do we go back home, and lick our wounds, metaphorically speaking or wallow in sadness by our loss? Or do we stay the week at the campground, and take my parents' offer to stay with them in their motor home and make the best out of this horrible situation? As part of my signature sign off on my social media video's "Make it a great day or not, the choice is yours!" Our choice was to practice what I preach about having a *positive mental attitude*. We decided to stay at Shaver Lake with the family, we used the pay phone to make our calls to the insurance company. Then I contacted my sister who would go to my home and pick up some clothing for Whit and me and then pick up clothes for Melinda and arrange a meeting place. My parents gave us $100 to buy items to get us through the next week while camping. We borrowed my dad's truck we headed back to Fresno to get those much-needed supplies.

At the end of the week, my parents rented a pontoon boat for the family to spend the last day on the lake together. This entire week I have wondered if my young nieces and nephews have really understood what happened to their Aunt Patti's motor home. Well, my answer came as I sat between my two nieces on the back of the pontoon boat fishing.

My six-year-old niece Tiffany said to me, 'Aunt Patti, your motorhome has burnt to the ground, and you have nothing'. It's as if the light bulb had finally gone off in her brain as to what had happened earlier in the week. At this point in my story, I know what you're thinking, 'she made this up, this cannot be true.' From God's lips to your ears, yes indeed it is all true, I even have the picture from the high patrol officer to prove it. Now a few moments ago, I called this a horrendous day. Was it really? No, it wasn't. It wasn't horrendous because no one died or even got injured throughout this entire journey. Did we all have homes, clothing, food and supplies we could return to? Yes, we did. The things that were destroyed, were just that, *things*. Eventually, those things were all replaced with more modern new things. To the best of the Highway Patrol's investigation as to the cause of the fire, which is really just a theory. They believed when one of the tires popped, since they were steel belted, that when a strip of the rubber left the tire, it cut the gas line leading to the generator. When I turned on the generator to run the air conditioner, the gas dripped out onto the hot exhaust pipe therefore starting the fire at the rear of the RV. Just a theory, we will never know for sure.

Now, how did this one day change my life? It gave me a bigger spectrum of what is important in this life. It's not about things; it's your loved ones. It's knowing that God really did have my back that day, just to be still and listen for his voice to direct me. It's also knowing that your family will wrap you in their loving arms, give you money to buy some clothing, make you up a little care package and make you a bed so you can still be camping in the Sierra's. You can always use a pay phone to call the insurance company. You're also knowing that your sister and her family will go to the trouble of going to your home and collect more clothing and supplies and will drive seven hours so you can make the best out of the entire strange event that has just taken place in your life. It's about several days after this event when your niece has her light bulb moment and makes her statement that I can smile and know I still have so much. Lastly, it is the ability to share this story with others and help them to find the positive in their bad days and times. At the end of the day, here I am 28 years later, safe, alive, smarter, wiser, and changed for the better.

Journey's Guide

1. Has there been an event in your life that you would consider has changed your life? If you have, in what ways has your life changed?

2. Do you consider these changes good or not, if not Why?

3. When faced with a dramatic event in your life, do you find yourself reaching out to other people or wanting to handle it on your own? Why do you feel this is the best course of action for you?

4. After a life-changing event has happened to you or someone close to you, are you or those you know, able at some point to find any positives to that experience? What positives could be learned and taken from that event.

CHAPTER EIGHT

A ROAD LESS TRAVELED. MY STORY OF LOST BEARINGS

'Sometimes we have to lose our way to find out what we really want, because we often ignore our needs until we are lost.'

By Leon Brown

As you may have noticed, in the way I shared that life-changing event of the destruction of my motor home, I was still able to stay upbeat about all that transpired. In the telling of that tale, what I didn't share in chapter six was the PTSD I have suffered from that event and the flashbacks I have when I have seen a recreational vehicle on fire on the side of the freeway. Through those flashback moments, I have always been able to find a way to work through them on my own. With this next major event in my life, there wasn't and still isn't anything light-hearted about it. I learned from this life-changing event that taking care of it on my own was not going to be an option.

As a natural born pathfinder before the age of fifty, I had never imagined losing my bearings. I had been on roads less traveled; however, those roads were the ones I could navigate by myself or with one of the trusted people in my life. As I have mentioned in previous chapters, due to unwise choices and the consequences that followed or other times in my life that life's challenges and obstacles came along. As I look back upon those times, I can see how these situations were preparing me for what was to come. So basically, what I am telling you is positive Patti hasn't always been so positive. I have had and continues to have down days and hard days. The difference now for me in this season of my life is thinking back on what the darkest days for me have been, and knowing I never want to go back there again.

So, in this chapter I will share with you how I lost my bearings, as I reflect on this part of my journey, I realize that losing my bearings was not a curse but a blessing in disguise. It allowed me to discover things about myself on the road that was behind me and the road I saw before me. This road less traveled, with all its twists and turns, was the crucible of my transformation, a journey where getting lost became the compass guiding me towards a truer, more authentic version of myself.

For many, I know you have experienced things that have been much more tragic and dramatic than what I have and will be sharing here. This isn't about comparing notes. This is about awareness and taking care of yourself in difficult situations. It's learning when you begin to feel that you are losing your bearings that it is time to reach out for help. There is nothing wrong with asking and getting help. It doesn't make you a weak person when you reach out for assistance. It makes you a stronger person.

I would like to share when I was a child, I spent time with my paternal grandmother. So, before our family visited my grandmother, dad would always remind us how we were to behave during our visit. My grandmother for most of the time seemed okay during most of our visits. With that being said, there were also many times that my grandmother seemed unhappy or angry. Often as a small child, I felt uneasy around her, aware I could make her angry. As I became a teenager and was able to drive, I made it a point to see if I could create a better relationship with my grandmother by doing projects for her and spending extra time with her. In some respects, I believe it did build a better relationship with her. But there still always seems to be that sharp edge to her. She passed away during my senior year in high school, which made me very glad that I had spent that extra time with her. Once I was in college, I would hear about people suffering with depression. I would also learn along the way about the different outcomes of people's depression, and I remember thinking how lucky I was that no one I knew had it. Famous last words.

When I was in my 30's, my dad asked me to talk with him. It was during this talk that he revealed that he was diagnosed with and suffered from depression. Thanks to some medication he was prescribed, he was able to function very well. This talk with my dad was a lightbulb moment for me in so many ways. I could see all through my life, those times I didn't know why he could blow up at a moment's notice or seem so sad and just sit in his chair staring at the TV. It was also during this talk that he let me know that my grandmother also suffered from depression which answered so many questions I had about her behavior. He also revealed that his doctor let him know that depression is hereditary and that his children and grandchildren could one day find themselves suffering from it. I remember thinking very briefly that will never happen to me. Again, famous last words.

As my journey on this path called life began to get busier and I moved into leadership roles on my campus, I began to find myself dealing with more uncertainty from all the different challenges life was bringing my way. I faced moments of self-doubt and questioned the wisdom of my choices. Before I knew it, it was as if I was running on a hamster wheel and couldn't figure out how to get off. Through it all, I kept a smile on my face and a motivating spirit whenever I was around others. I mean come on, I'm Positive Patti. If I thought the challenges of my professional life were difficult, they were nothing compared to the challenges that came when my dad was diagnosed with prostate cancer. This is where my family began to learn about this horrific disease. For the next five years, what started out as prostate cancer became bladder cancer and finally bone cancer. Just let me add right here, right now, Cancer Sucks. As the oldest child, I have always had this inherent desire to make things as good as possible for everyone, especially in difficult situations. When it came down to the final year of my dad's life, keeping a balance of teaching and helping my parents unbeknownst to me at the time was taking its toll.

I now know I wasn't taking care of myself while all of this was happening. I was giving and doing for everyone else and forgot about taking care of me in the process. I know many of you can totally relate to all of this. For the final two weeks of my dad's life, I was basically with him 24 / 7 and over the past four to five days of his life, our entire immediate family were with my parents' night and day until his passing in September 2010. Finalizing his funeral arrangements with my mom, calling loved ones, officiating his celebration of life service, helping my mom with many of the details that go along with paperwork after your spouse has passed, attending grief group classes with her plus continuing to teach. I believed I was managing it all beautifully. That was until almost three months later the final day of school before winter break.

As I was getting ready to go home for the day, I thought I was having a heart attack. I was forty-nine years old, getting ready to turn fifty in another month. My dad had his first heart attack at age forty-seven. My chest felt tight, I thought my heart was going to beat out of my chest, and I was short of breath. I then did what you should never do, I drove myself to the hospital emergency room fifteen minutes away. As soon as I entered the ER, I let them know I thought I was having a heart attack and before I knew it, I was hooked up to an EKG machine, plus having all kinds of bloodwork, tests and scans done, then checked into the hospital for further testing and evaluation. Two days later, it was determined that I had had a major anxiety / panic attack. The cardiologist felt it was brought on by the grief of losing my dad and even though I was in grief counseling, I hadn't really dealt with his death and all that came before it and afterwards.

The following month, I found myself crying all the time, which was very unusual for me. I was unmotivated to do anything which was also unusual for me. I wasn't looking forward to celebrating my fiftieth birthday, which was highly unusual for me not to want to celebrate my birthday, especially this important milestone. Somehow, I made it through the month of January and made the best of celebrating my birthday. A week later, however, I couldn't get myself out of bed. I just wanted to sleep all the time. I called in sick from school each morning, gave some very brief lesson plans, rolled over and went back to sleep. I wasn't showering or eating. In my brain, I felt as if my brain was on hyper speed, and I couldn't concentrate or stop the words from songs playing repeatedly. My loved ones had never seen me like this before and were extremely concerned about my welfare. No matter what they tried to do to make me feel better, nothing seemed to help.

After a week of this madness in my brain and body, there was a voice I heard that said 'if you were to die today, no one would care.' That scared me, I knew I was in trouble and needed help. I had done enough suicide prevention with my students over the years to know I wasn't going to be able to fix this on my own. I immediately called my doctor's office to see if I could get in to see him, *urgently*.

The receptionist said he could see me in a week. The next words that came out of my mouth shocked me. I heard myself say, "you don't understand, if I don't get in to see him today, I don't know if I will be alive tomorrow.'

The receptionist asked me to hold on for one moment. Before I knew it, I heard her telling me to come in. As soon as I hung up the phone, I then began to write down everything I had been experiencing so I could give that to my doctor. I don't even remember driving to his office, I only remember checking in with the receptionist and being led to a chair in the back office, then being handed a clipboard with several pages of questions to answer. After reading the first five questions on page one, I heard my inner voice screaming 'they think I'm crazy.' With that in mind I began to answer the questions on page two, my inner voice switched to 'they think I'm depressed.' Answering 'myself with 'I can't be depressed, I'm Positive Patti'. It was then that I remembered that conversation that dad and I had had all those years earlier, about depression running in the family and it was hereditary.

Once I completed the questionnaire, I was taken to a room to wait for my doctor to see me. As soon as he walked in, I began to cry. I took out the piece of paper I had written down about all I was experiencing and everything that was happening to me and he very gently said, 'I don't need to see that paper to know that something is terribly wrong.' You see, he had known me for many years, I had taught his children, anytime there was a physical ailment that had come my way over those years, he had always known me to be upbeat, positive, motivational, and keeping a positive mental attitude. This was a Patti he had never experienced before. He knew I had entered some type of dark rabbit hole, and I was going to need help navigating it.

Journey's Guide

Has there been a time in your life that you felt you had lost your bearings? Write down what that experience felt like for you.

Creativity Time

This road less traveled chapter for me became a canvas on which I painted my lost bearings experience. On this page below, take a pen or pencil, close your eyes and begin to draw around the page. After a few minutes, open your eyes and look at the design. With colored pencils, pens or markers, create a colorful canvas out of this design you have just created. Notice the beauty that has been created by adding color to the design. What does this say to you about your journey?

CHAPTER NINE

NAVIGATING THE ABYSS

'All of us are constantly navigating the abyss between two great unknowns: what we think of ourselves and what others think of us.'

By Sally Rooney

As I begin to write this chapter, and I reflect on my journey, I have come to realize that losing my bearings was not a curse but a blessing in disguise. The road less traveled, with all its twists and turns, became my crucible for the beginning of my transformation, a journey where getting lost became the compass guiding me towards a truer, more authentic version of myself. Each twist and turn have also become a chapter in the story of my personal growth. As I sat in my doctor's office talking with him on what had been happening, my doctor said he wanted to get some blood work done. Then came the big question, he asked me 'are you willing to talk to someone and get some help?' There was no hesitation on my part, I immediately agreed. He had a therapist friend that he would call and see if he could see me later that same day. Three hours later, I found myself sitting in the therapist's office.

Up to this point in my life, I had never been in a therapist office before. I used to watch the Bob Newhart show where he was a therapist, but that's as close as I had ever been to seeing a therapist. As I think back to that moment in time, I was a shell of the person I had always known myself to be. It's as if I was a zombie. I sat there staring at different objects in his office trying to figure out how I got to this point. How did this happen? What am I doing here? How is this supposed to help me? How long will it take before I am back to my old self. What will my family and friends think if they find out I'm here?

Since I had never had this type of experience before, I had no idea how this was supposed to work. So, I just sat there looking at the therapist, finally, after what seemed like an eternity, he asked me about what was going on. I proceeded to take out my list that I had written for my doctor and began to read it to him. Once I had finished reading the list, he asked me how those things were different from how I normally would be. As I sat there, thinking about his question, I began to answer.

I felt like my brain, my mouth and the words coming out of my mouth were all in slow motion. It was in this moment that I realized that I had personally entered new territory for me professionally, physically, spiritually and emotionally. I had entered the realm of mental health and needed help navigating this part of my journey. I recognized that this part of my expedition was going to be challenging terrain.

I soon discovered that the tricky side of mental health is not a straight path forward. It is a convoluted maze where shadows of anxiety, panic attacks, depression, and other mental health challenges loom. Sitting in the therapist's office I found myself beginning to hesitate to share my story with him due to the fear of judgment, fear of people finding out I was seeing a therapist and thinking I was crazy. More judgement. By the end of this first session, I must admit, I felt like it had done nothing for me and wasn't looking forward to coming back the next week. However, with the following events, I discovered that acknowledging my situation was the first crucial step towards my understanding and healing.

The following day, I received a call from my doctor to come to his office to go over the results of my blood tests. They discovered that I had zero estrogen in my system. Ten years earlier, I had to have a hysterectomy due to years of battling endomitosis. Even though I still had my ovaries, something was happening that they weren't producing any estrogen. This was a huge light bulb moment for both of us as to what was partially going on with me mentally and physically.

With this newfound knowledge, he was able to prescribe me medication that almost immediately helped me mentally. Hallelujah! As happy as I was to discover this missing part of my mental health journey, the pathfinder in me needed to find out why I couldn't get over the anxiety and panic attacks I was still experiencing. I was still holding on to hope that the therapist could help me find those missing pieces. After attending eight weeks of sessions in therapy, I wish I could tell you right here and right now that those missing pieces were discovered, and I went my merry way. But sadly, I can't. I received nothing from this therapist; I chose not to continue with him.

Through my own research, I began to learn that mental health is not a weakness but a testament to the strength required to confront one's inner demons. This part of my journey involved confronting uncomfortable truths, and unpacking layers of emotions. Although daunting, it became a space for my self-discovery and acceptance. Since I had left the professional therapist, I discovered what had been before me this entire time, which was the grief counseling that I was attending with mom. Did I have blinders on? When they were talking about the process of grief. My view up to this point is that I was taking my mom to grief counseling to help her, not me.

My Aha! moment happened the following week in grief counseling class. Our incredible grief counselor Nancy's lesson that week was teaching us how to basically navigate the abyss of grief with a shift in perspective. With Nancy's help, advise and support, she became my guiding light, an essential compass that offered strategies for coping and tools for resilience. Again, almost immediately with this discovery, I realized that reaching out for help was not a sign of weakness but a courageous act of self-love. With Nancy's encouragement, I also began participating in a program with the hospice Chaplin Cal. Over the next two years, I attended grief counseling with Nancy once a week and worked with Cal once a week. Not only did I find myself learning the tools to help me out of this grief and mental health abyss, but it also became a bridge connecting me to a community that understood the nuances of the struggle.

This journey is not solitary. In sharing my story with others in the grief groups, we dismantled the isolations that often accompanies grief and mental health battles. In a sense, we became unified in our collective journey towards healing. As I continued to navigate the abyss, I recognized that grief and mental health are not a destination but an ongoing exploration. It is one that demands patience, self-compassion, and a commitment to breaking down the barriers. My journey through the labyrinth of grief and mental health has become a testament to the transformative power of understanding, resilience, and the unwavering belief that, even in the darkest moments, there is a path toward healing and hope. I can now say without shame or embarrassment 'I am Patti Stueland, and I suffer from depression.'

Journey's Guide

1. Write about the type of 'Abyss' have you faced or are facing now?

2. With that abyss, how did you navigate it or how are you navigating it?

3. Who are those individuals in your life that became, are becoming or could be your 'guiding light'.

4. Write down as many words as you can think of that describe what an abyss sounds like, looks like, feels like and smells like to you.

5. Write down as many positive words as you can think of that describe what navigating the abyss sounds, looks, feels and smells like to you.

CHAPTER TEN

EMBRACING HELP, A PATH TO HEALING

'Healing is a matter of time, but it is sometimes also a matter of opportunity.'

By Hippocrates

As I have already mentioned before, embracing help is not a sign of weakness, but a courageous stride toward healing. As you read in Chapter 8, as soon as I reached out to my doctor, that is where I began my journey to embracing help. This was extremely difficult for me. I had always been a very independent person. I could figure it out or do it all on my own. It wasn't an ego thing; it was not wanting to bother anyone else with my own stuff. However, I was all about wanting to help others and encouraging them to call on me for help. As a society, we often valorize the notion of independence, perpetuating the myth that strength lies in weathering storms alone. As you just read in the last chapter, my own narrative shifted when I encountered the transformative power of reaching out for help. It was a pivotal realization that marked the beginning of a profound healing process.

The one thing I did do and had done for a number of years and continue to do to so, is to acknowledge my previous grief and mental health crisis. I had a couple of trusted individuals in my life that when things at school were getting the best of me, all I needed to do was to go to them, tell them what was going on and get it off my chest. I wasn't looking for answers or solutions to the situation, I just needed to say it out loud. Many times, I discovered the answer immediately from saying it out loud or at least I felt much better expressing it and I could move forward.

Do you have those trusted individuals in your life? Some of the very valuable lessons I learned from the incredible grief counselor Nancy, was tears are healing, grief storms can hit you at any time and to just go with it, there is no shame in asking for help, and remember to take care of you. That last thing I just mentioned about taking care of you was a mind-blowing concept for me when Nancy spoke about it. I realized that before my dad's death, and after his death, I had forgotten to take care of me. I was so concerned for my family, my friends, my students, my school faculty and staff and for everyone else. Not only did I have zero estrogen in my system, but I had also completely drained my self-love and self-care tank.

Self-love and self-care weren't even on my radar. After grief class one night, Nancy asked if we could talk. It was during this conversation that I was experiencing burn out. She wanted me to think about the things that brought me joy and happiness. What hobbies did I have, what was on my bucket list. It was this 'homework' assignment that became an important and vital part of my path to healing. This pathfinder took this assignment very seriously and discovered that I needed to create a balance between work and free time with things I enjoyed.

Nancy suggested looking into some possible elective classes at our local junior college. This was another step forward on my path to healing. I had always wanted to learn how to play the piano and saw in the college catalog of classes a beginning piano class. I registered for the class, and this is where I began to refill my self-love and self-care tank. I was by far the oldest person in the class, and I didn't care. I liked my instructor, and I loved learning this new skill, I even bought a keyboard so I could be sure to practice at home and take it with me on a couple of camping trips. Those Monday and Wednesday night classes were just what I needed to help me get through the week. It was practicing at home one night when I realized that taking this piano class was the first class I had ever taken for pure enjoyment and enrichment. Up to that point all the classes, workshops, conferences, plus retreats I had ever done before were all related to my work. When the semester was coming to an end, I knew I needed and wanted to find another class to take. As soon as I could look at next semester's offerings, I discovered the next course. Beginners drawing, up to this point I was self-taught with the drawings I would do. I remember doing my first drawing around four years old. Once again, I was the oldest person in the class and I didn't care, loved my instructor and absolutely loved the entire process of how to draw all kinds of things. Again, these Tuesday and Thursday evening classes got me through the week mentally and spiritually.

By the end of that school year after taking those elective classes, I was so much stronger when it came to my mental health. It was also at this same time that I knew after two years of grief counseling, I was strong enough not only mentally, but spiritually as well. My self-care and self-love tank wasn't filled, but it was on its way to getting topped off.

I knew it was time to spread my wings and forge my way back out into the world without going to years old grief counseling any longer. One of the final areas that my grief counselor Nancy recognized in me was the loss of passion with my teaching career. By this point in time, I was fifty-three years old, and my Dad had been gone for three years. My life had changed in so many ways.

Our immediate family unit had changed dramatically, the administration on my campus had changed (not for the good) and I changed teaching assignments. That's when I seriously began to look at retiring from teaching in my mid-fifties. I had always thought that I would be teaching at least until I was in my mid-sixties, however this was when I began to discover God had other plans for my future. With a new spirit and attitude, I began my 29th year in education on a high note. One of my dear colleagues, Josh, was the wood shop instructor and he had invited me to come to his after-school woodshop program that met twice a week. My dad and I had done woodworking projects for years, so this invitation from Josh was exciting. Once I began taking that class, I knew I would be set for this school year on participating in something that was just for me. Once more I'm the oldest person in the class and didn't care. In fact, the class was filled with our high school students, and they thought it was cool that one of the teachers was taking a class with them and learning alongside them. Overall, it was an okay school year. It was during this school year that my very dear friend, Sue, taught me how to 'Zen doodle.' Each time I found myself getting anxious, stressed or nervous about something, she wanted me to take a piece of paper and just start drawing.

It didn't need to have a purpose or a reason. There were no mistakes when you Zen doodled. Just go with the flow. Draw symbols, lines, letters, numbers, whatever seemed right in that moment, just draw. Using a pen, pencil, markers, it didn't matter. If I wanted to color it with crayons, paints, chalks, markers or use the writing utensil to create the design and color, it's all good. Wow. Zen doodling was an amazing form of stress relieving for me. My students would see some of my Zen doodles on my desk and it would create a whole new connection with them when they talk with me about the design and color. Many of them would then share with me things they had drawn or created. I could see a wonderful sense of pride coming from them as they shared these treasured items with me. And in return, I also felt a sense of pride in myself when I received their compliments on what I had created.

Taking the woodshop class was the highlight during this school year. I loved taking scraps of wood and turning it into something useful; a writing pen, a birdhouse, a Christmas tree and many more fun and creative items. As I approached the final month of that school year, there was an incident that took place with a student. I caught them violating and breaking a school rule. I won't go into any specific details, except to say, this student and their parents created a scenario of this event that took place that was not even close to the truth. I then realized in the span of one school day, out of the past twenty-eight years of teaching, that this one false statement by a student could possibly cost me my job. The district and Town police had to get involved in an investigation and I was afraid I might be put on administrative leave. I could not believe this was happening; I wasn't put on administrative leave thanks to my administration and district police going to bat for me. I felt extremely lucky.

On the final day of school, I had to go to the district office for a hearing on this case. Up to this point, no one was allowed to let me know what was going on. Talk about high anxiety and panic attacks. When I showed up for the hearing, I was overwhelmed by what I saw. I saw our campus security, district security, and some of the school office staff all there to testify on my behavior.

After I gave my statement, I needed to leave the area and would be notified of the outcome later that day. As I drove home and realized that I was now on summer break, I also realized something else, my teaching days were over. By the time I got home, I was an emotional mess, I knew I needed to teach at least one more year to turn fifty-five years old and get my thirty years in to receive a somewhat decent retirement pension.

I had the next nine weeks of summer break to figure out how I was going to get through that final year. I spent that summer at my happy place, Pismo Beach on the central coast of California and basically got my act together. By the time that first day of school came around I had decided to put everything I had into making it the best year ever. It was one of my best school years ever. In fact, a majority of the faculty, staff and students kept saying 'you're back and better than ever, retire now, why? Reminding myself daily that I knew it would be my final year, and that I was more than capable of putting it all out there.

As I helped to coordinate and organize the final graduation ceremony that I would be a part of, I saw this ceremony as my own graduation ceremony. Something that had started as a dream as a six-year-old, becoming the first female on both sides of my family to graduate with a bachelor's degree, and fulfilling that dream of being a teacher, I was darn proud of myself at that graduation ceremony. Yes, I had indeed embraced help to get me here and I knew all of it was part of the path to my healing. I also knew at this point, God had other plans for me. It was time to discover my retirement motto.

'Life in an Adventure, so enjoy the Journey'.

Journey's Guide

Creative Journey: On this page create a map of what the path of healing would look like. Name the starting point, name the stops along the path, and how that healing path ends on this page. Be creative with your titles, colors, and design. This is your path of healing, go for it and have fun with it.

CHAPTER ELEVEN

LIFE'S AND ADVENTURE, ENJOY THE JOURNEY

Life should not be a journey to the grave with the intention of arriving safely in a pretty and well-preserved body, but rather to skid in broadside in a cloud of smoke, thoroughly used up, totally worn out and loudly proclaiming 'Wow, what a ride.'

by Hunter. S. Thompson

Quotes and mantras have always been important in my life. When I retired, I wanted and needed to create a mantra for this new chapter of my life that I was about to experience. Since I was six years old, my goal was to become a teacher, that goal was achieved. Now after thirty-five years of athletic coaching and teaching, that part of my life had come to an end. At least that is what I thought at the time. I saw many signs in stores and on websites that would say *Life's an Adventure or Enjoy the Journey*. I related so much to both sayings that I chose to put them together and they have become my retirement mantra. At this point in the book, you have already seen that quotes and sayings are important in my life. They inspire me, and they motivate me and they are a part of what brings passion and purpose into my life. When I retired from teaching, there was a moment in time where I thought, what the heck did you just do? Teaching was all I ever wanted to do, and teaching is all I had ever done. If I wasn't a teacher any longer, who was I? What was my purpose moving forward? That's when I had my Aha! Moment.

'I could do anything I wanted to do'

Little did I know what God had in store for me. My retirement adventure / journey began with an article in the Sunday Parade Magazine article talking about the second act people aged fifty-five and older. It talked about the new jobs and careers they began during their retirement. I saw something called a life cycle celebrant in the article and decided to go to the website and check it. I know, right now you are thinking exactly what I thought at the time, what is that? Basically, what I like to say is it's a person who officiates ceremonies from the womb to the tomb.

For twenty of the thirty years I taught, I had loved being an Activities Director. Becoming a life cycle celebrant would partly involve the part of being an activities director. I loved creating and being a part of a celebration. After attending online classes for a year, I graduated and that is when 'Life's Special Moments' officiating was born.

My officiating niche is in weddings and funerals. Some of you may be wondering about how funerals or as I prefer to call them A Celebration of Life Services would be part of my niche. This was born out of a very sad and tough time in my life and the life of my family. A year before my dad passed away from a valiant five-year battle with several cancers, I had attended the funeral service for a dear family friend. During the service for this incredible human being, you could tell throughout the service that the officiant knew nothing about our friend; including how to pronounce his last name. After the service I went to visit my dad since he was too sick at this time to attend. I told him of my sadness about the funeral service and asked him if he had thought about who he wanted to officiate his service. He looked me right in my eyes and said 'you.' That took me by complete surprise. 'I would be honored,' was my reply.

Over the next several months I began to put his celebration of life service together. I practiced repeatedly, I wanted to make him proud and not get over emotional. Two months before he passed away, I had finished his service and asked him one day when we were sitting outside, if he would like to hear his celebration of life service and his response was 'I would like that'. He sat bundled up in his favorite reclining yard chair and I sat at the picnic table and conducted his celebration of life service for him I was proud of not crying as I spoke about my dad's imminent passing. When I had finished, I looked at him to see and hear his reaction. He looked at me, smiled, saying 'that's exactly what I want'. To me that was an impressive gift. Two months later, in the cemetery chapel, packed with family and friends, I officiated my dad's celebration of life service. Once again, I never shed a tear until the service was over, and from the compliments I received, realized that God had given me another gift.

In the last seven years since being retired and became a Life-Cycle Celebrant, I have spoken at and performed at many family and friends' celebrations of life's services. I have also had the honor and privilege to officiate several former students and friends' wedding services. It had been quite an adventure and a wonderful part of my journey. The adventures and journeys continued as I also began my number one retirement goal of selling my beloved home and traveling the United States full time in my motorhome. In the past four years, I have covered approximately 70% of the 48 contiguous states. If it weren't for Covid and the lockdown, I would probably be 100% traveled. Upon my sixtieth, I felt there was still so much more I wanted and needed to do and had to offer.

With help and training from some mentors, my business Pathways with Patti was created. I am a motivational/inspirational speaker, transformational coach helping people to discover or rediscover their passion and purpose. I am a two-time Amazon bestselling co-author, TEDx speaker, podcaster, I own my own travel agent business called 'Pathfinder Patti Travel' and as you are reading it right now, a fully-fledged author of my own book *'Living Your Best Dash'*. The point of all of this is not for me to brag upon myself. However, looking at it in writing right now, I'm pretty darn proud of myself. I want it to serve as an example of what is possible for you. The adventure and the journey doesn't have to end unless you choose for it to end. I believe when you feel you have reached the point in your life where you know it all and have seen it all, you begin to die. Personally, I never want to get to that point. Just as *Hunter S. Thompson* said in his quote at the beginning of this chapter.

> *'I want to be 'thoroughly used up, totally worn out and loudly proclaiming 'wow what a ride'.*

My adventure and journey are not done yet and neither is yours. Choose to live a life filled with passion and purpose until your last breath. *Your life matters, Life is an adventure, and I want you to enjoy the journey.*

Journey's Guide

1. How does the perspective of viewing life as an adventure impact on your overall attitude and approach to challenges?

2. Write about a personal experience where embracing the journey rather than focusing solely on the destination made a significant difference in your life?

3. In what ways can adopting the mindset of life's adventure enhance creativity and critical thinking skills in your daily living?

4. Do you believe that enjoying the journey is equally important in both personal and professional aspects of life? Why or why

5. Reflection time: Take 15 minutes to journal about a recent experience where you faced a challenge. Explore how embracing the journey, rather than fixating on the outcome, influenced your emotions and decision-making during that time.

CHAPTER TWELVE

MAKE IT A GREAT DAY OR NOT, THE CHOICE IS YOURS

'Don't wait for someday to start living because someday may never come. Make the choice right now to be happy and live life to the fullest.'

by Robert Tew

When I started my twenty-year run as an activity director, one of my duties was to do the morning announcements. When I was growing up, there was a news anchor named Jerry Dunphy and each night when he would begin his part of the news, he would begin it by saying, 'From the desert to the sea, to all of Southern California, a good evening.' Then there was news anchor Walter Cronkite who would end his broadcast with the quote, 'And that's the way it is,' followed by the date of the broadcast. Serving at Vista Campana Middle as the activities director and knowing that these sixth, seventh and eighth grade students would need to listen to me each school morning to start their school day, I knew I needed and wanted to have something to capture their attention at the beginning of the announcements and finish it off with something profound for them to think about.

To create my opening statement of the morning was easy, it was inspired by Robin Williams from his movie 'Good morning, Vietnam. So, I began each morning's announcements with a very happy, hearty, and enthusiastic 'Good Morning Bulldogs'! When I moved to the feeder high school, the greeting was 'Good Morning Cougars'!" To end each morning's announcements, I would say 'Make it a great day or not, the choice is yours'. It didn't give the name of the person who said it, I just knew when I saw it, it was a light bulb moment for me. We all have choices to make which you read about in Chapter 4.

I know for some; this statement may not ring true for them. There are those who feel like the word 'choices' is overpowering and not empowering. As with everything I am mentioning in this book, my choice is to live a life that is full and abundant. It is my hope that while you are reading this book, that you will begin or continue to see the many 'choices' you have available when you have an attitude of gratitude and believe it, to achieve it. It isn't always easy and some days you just aren't feeling it and that's ok.

As I have mentioned before, have your pity party, just don't pitch a tent and stay there. Feel your feelings, learn from them, and use the lesson to move forward. So, the question is now, how do we even begin to have a great day? Well let me show you: Seize the Day: Carpe diem. Seize the days, boys. Make your lives extraordinary.' Dead Poets Society: Live your life with Intention. Every day we have opportunities. When you choose to embrace each present moment with intention and savor those life offerings, you are creating a life of positivity and fulfillment. You can transform your power of choice. You can make each day extraordinary, giving yourself a life of limitless possibilities of living life to the fullest.

The Choice is Ours: 'Every test in our life makes us bitter or better, every problem comes to break us or make us. The choice is ours whether we become a VICTIM or VICTOR.' www.livelifehappy.com

Our everyday surroundings hold the possibility with a variety of choices. Choices that shape our experiences, color our perspectives, and ultimately define the story of our lives. We have the power to choose our response to events, to steer the course of our emotions, and shape the reality we wish to inhabit.

Embrace the Here and Now: *Whatever could have been or should have been, doesn't matter. This Moment is here and now for you to live.* @masteringlawsofattraction

The notion of someday often casts a shadow over the present, taking us into a type of mirage that life's true essence lies in the distant future. Break the chains of procrastination and embrace what life is offering you now. Now is when you can create your dreams, learn, and grow about what brings you joy, happiness and fulfillment. Look upon each new day as a blank page. Take that pen and begin the work of bringing those dreams and goals to life.

From The Power of Positive Choices:

'If you don't like the road you're walking, start paving another one'
By Dolly Parton

Choice is more than mere decision-making, it's a declaration of intent, a powerful affirmation we put out into the world. When we choose happiness, we defy the pull of negativity and create a chain reaction of positive energy. That energy then leaves us and creates a ripple effect that moves beyond us to positively affect an unlimited number of other lives.

Our choices create optimism and inspiration. These are just a few of the ways we can make it a great day with the choices we make. The list could continue here but now they will be featured in the upcoming chapters. I encourage you to seize the day, to step out of the shadows of someday and to embrace the power of choice. With an open heart and an eager spirit, make the choice to be happy and live life to the fullest. I want you to embark on a journey of empowerment, transformation, and the fulfilment of a well-lived life.

Journey's Guide

How can your mindset and attitude influence the outcome of your day?

1. What are some proactive steps you can take to turn a challenging day into a great one?
2. Reflect on a time when your attitude significantly impacted your day. What did you learn from that experience?
3. In what ways can you empower yourself to make each day a positive and fulfilling experience?

Time to get Creative.

Gather magazines, scissors, glue, and a poster board.

Create a vision board illustrating the elements that represent a great day for you.

Include images, quotes, and symbols that inspire positivity and motivation.

Daily Affirmation Writing:

Set aside a few minutes each morning to write positive affirmations.

Focus on aspects that will contribute to making your day great.

Carry these affirmations with you and repeat them throughout the day for reinforcement.

CHAPTER THIRTEEN

I'M H-A-P-P-Y!!!

'I, not events, have the power to make me happy or unhappy today. I can choose which it shall be. Yesterday is dead, tomorrow hasn't arrived yet. I have just one day, today, and I'm going to be happy in it.'
by Groucho Marx

When I was attending the Cal Poly Physical Education Workshop one summer, I attended a week-long class that was taught by two extremely inspirational, motivational and phenomenal women: Pam Allor and Charlene Eichelberger. During that weeklong course, we learned how to create a classroom of inclusion, giving 'happies and the meaning of 'HAPPY' embracing the gift of today and creating a light of joy and choice.

Groucho Marx says it perfectly in his quote mentioned at the beginning of this chapter. It serves as a beacon of empowerment. I, not events, have the power to make me happy or unhappy today. I can choose which it should be. This simple statement holds a universal truth, the Power of choice and the control over our emotions.

In this chapter we will journey into the heart of this wisdom, exploring how we can transform the potential of our mindset, the art of living in the present, and the resounding truth that happiness is, indeed, a choice. Let's take a closer look at some of the ways we have a choice.

1. Mastery of Self: Groucho Marx's words unveil the mastery that lies within us; the Mastery over our reactions and emotions. This mastery isn't out of reach for any of us. It is a tangible reality that emerges when we recognize that we are the ones in shaping our experiences. We are not at the mercy of events. Rather, we are the authors of our responses, and the pathfinders of our emotional life's path.

2. Power of Perspective: As we travel our life's path, unexpected events can happen at any time. Some of these events bring joy, while others cast shadows of challenges. It's not the events themselves that dictate our emotional state; it's our perspective that influences us the most. When we view events as opportunities for growth, as chapters in our personal journey, we can transform the mundane into the magnificent.

3. The Power of Now: Groucho Marx's wisdom, is an invitation to embrace the power of now: to completely put ourselves in the present moment with all that it offers us. All the things that happened yesterday whether they were positive or negative, and all the things that might happen tomorrow, all pale in comparison to the beauty that is today. The power of now is the power of choice. We can choose to fill our reality with positivity, gratitude, and the intention to savor life's offerings.

4. The Gift of Choice: We can choose how we respond to life's twists and turns, whether with resentment or with grace, with despair or with hope. This gift goes beyond circumstance, placing the reins of our emotional well-being directly in our hands. Our emotional landscape transforms into a realm where we choose to bring in joy, peace and contentment.

5. Breaking Free from the Past: The past often casts a shadow over the present, with memories, regrets, and unfulfilled aspirations. It is time for us to break free from this shadow, to recognize that yesterday's history has no bearing on today's narrative. We can choose to release the weight of the past and acknowledge that the dawn of a new day offers us a clean slate, a new chapter waiting to be written.

6. Symphony of Gratitude: The choice to be happy is intertwined with the threads of gratitude. When we focus on life's blessings, big and small, we bring into our reality a symphony of thankfulness. Gratitude shifts our attention from what's lacking in our lives to what's abundant, from what's wrong to what's right to transform the mundane moments in our lives into jewels of happiness.

7. Madness of Waiting: How often do we postpone happiness, waiting for the arrival of a particular event or circumstance? We need to remind ourselves that tomorrow isn't guaranteed to anyone. The future is filled with uncertainty, and waiting for happiness to arrive with a particular future event robs us of the precious gift of now. Happiness is not a destination; it's a choice that colors our journey.

8. Embrace Imperfection: The pursuit of happiness is not an endeavor devoid of challenges or imperfections. It's a conscious decision to embrace life's imperfections, to find beauty in the flawed, and to come through adversity with resilience. When we approach life's imperfections with a heart filled with acceptance, we pave the way for genuine happiness to flourish.

9. Cultivate a Positive Outlook: The choice to be happy is a declaration of our intention to cultivate a positive outlook. It's a commitment to view challenges as steppingstones, setbacks as opportunities for growth, uncertainties as an invitation to explore uncharted territories. A positive outlook serves to draw experiences with our chosen frequency of joy.

10. Art of Mindfulness: The foundation of choosing happiness is grounded in mindfulness and is the art of being present with an open heart and a curious mind. Mindfulness allows us to enjoy life's richness, to relish the simple pleasures, and to experience each moment as a unique gift.

Through mindfulness, we create our reality and build a life that mirrors our inner landscape of joy. Groucho Marx's quote reminds me of how transformative the choice of happiness can be in our lives right now in this moment. It reminds each of us to become aware of our emotional reality, recognize that the power to shape our experiences resides within us. As we explore and navigate our lives, let us remember that happiness isn't an elusive pursuit; it's a conscious choice that resonates with the heartbeat of the present. By embracing this wisdom, we become the cocreators of a life filled with positivity inspiration, and the belief that today, and every day, is a new chapter waiting to be written with the words of our chosen happiness.

Journey's Guide

1. On a scale of 1 to 10, 1 being extremely unhappy to 10 and being extremely happy, where would you rate how happy you are overall with your life?

   Why did you give yourself that rating?

   Whatever rating you gave yourself when it comes to being happy, what do you need to raise or maintain that rating?

2. On a scale of 1 to 10, 1 being 'not in the present moment ever' to 10 being constantly in the present moment)

   What rating do you give yourself in this present moment?

   What is the reason for this rating?

   What will it take for you to be 'more' in this present moment? Or maintain being in the moment?

3. Write down five things you are grateful and thankful for right now.

4. What is it from your past that you need to release?

5. What mindfulness techniques can you practice helping you cultivate a positive outlook?

How about we now break down what

H.A.P.P.Y. means?

It's all in the following chapters.

CHAPTER FOURTEEN

HEALTHY

'It is health that is real wealth and not pieces of gold and silver.
By Mahatma Gandhi

As someone who has battled with my weight my entire life, 'Patti Fatty' was the nickname I was called as a child by some unkind children. Being a physical education teacher, I know the importance and the struggles that go along with being healthy.

With each decade I have been blessed to live, I have also learned that being 'healthy' just isn't about your weight. It encompasses your mind, body, and soul. In this chapter, we will look at your health from not only a physical standpoint, but emotionally, and spiritually. I know that when we are healthy in each of those areas of our life, which is when we are and can be at our happiest. Being healthy in mind, body and spirit is a true treasure and not one to taken for granted. In today's world we often find that the pursuit of wealth often takes stage. Mahatma Gandhi's profound wisdom in his above quote can serve us as a guiding light.

No matter what part of the world you may live in, the worth of good health is invaluable. When we see our health as being a true treasure, that is when we begin to recognize how nurturing our wellbeing ignites a wealth of positivity, inspiration, and the fulfilment of a life well-lived.

Health is the cornerstone upon which a life filled with vitality, joy and purpose are built. It is a treasure that surpasses the value of any material possession because it enriches every aspect of our existence. As I mentioned in previous chapters, I discovered this the hard way when I was burned out on teaching and discovered I was 'burned out' on life. I had forgotten to take care of myself, I had forgotten to make my overall health a priority, and I had forgotten that My Life Mattered.

As I have mentioned, the concept of health as wealth goes beyond physical wellness, in the areas of mental, emotional, and spiritual health. I have learned that it is a holistic approach that recognizes the intricate interplay between mind,
body and soul. When these areas are in harmony with one another, we can sense a wholeness and fulfilment in our lives that elevates our life experiences to a level beyond what we believe to be possible. Imagine a life abundant in wealth, yet marred by ailments and limitations.

Now envision a life where vitality, energy and wellness serve as the foundation of every endeavor. This is the area I want you to really take in. This is where life is fueled by real wealth and health. When our bodies are vibrant, our minds are sharp, and our spirits uplifted, everything we pursue becomes one filled with enthusiasm and purpose. Heath becomes the foundation of a life brimming with fulfillment. Did you know there is a ripple effect when it comes to our health? When we tap into the treasure of health, it radiates outward, and it creates a ripple effect that extends to every part of our lives. When we prioritize our wellbeing, we inspire others to do the same. Our energy, positivity, and zest for life becomes contagious, creating a mindset that values health as the ultimate wealth.

This ripple effect transforms families, communities, and society. It is what fosters a culture of vitality and wellbeing. How cool is that? Good health empowers us to pursue our dreams, ambitions, and aspirations. When our bodies are strong and our minds clear, we now have what is needed to overcome obstacles and embrace challenges. Health equips us with resilience and stamina to navigate the journey towards our goals, helping us to embark on each new endeavor with great determination. Imagine your health as a boundless reservoir of energy that fuels every step of our journey. This allows us to seize opportunities, conquer challenges, and enjoy the beauty of life's experiences. We find that our days are then filled with vigor, our actions have purpose, and our hearts are filled with/gratitude for the gift of vitality. As you may have already noticed throughout this book, I continue to mention the importance of selfcare. Prioritizing health entails embracing the art of self-care, nurturing ourselves with kindness, nourishment, and rest.

This practice isn't one of self-indulgence, but of self-respect. It is a recognition that our bodies deserve to be treated with respect and care. By embracing selfcare, we cultivate a sense of worthiness that begins from within and radiates positivity and inspires others to honor their own wellbeing.

Never forget that you are worth it. When we are healthy in our mind, body, and spirit, we have freedom. Good health grants us the freedom to explore the world around us. It allows us to embark on adventures, discover new horizons, and immerse ourselves in diverse experiences. When we are free from physical limitations, we can journey to new places, engage in a variety of activities and create incredible memories of living life fully. Health is a gift, one that often goes unnoticed until something happens to us valuable artifacts. We must recognize the worth of our health.

Every mindful choice we make, every act of self-care, and every moment of gratitude becomes a tribute to the treasure that is our wellbeing. As we navigate life's journey, health is the compass that guides us towards longevity and vitality. It's the key to a life marked by quality, rather than just quantity. It's a gift that warrants cherishing and nurturing, just as we treasure precious jewels and artifacts. When we invest in our health, we gift ourselves with the opportunity to experience the full spectrum of life's wonders, from as I like to say, 'womb to tomb'. Remember that health is a true treasure. As we journey through our path of life, let us also remember that prioritizing health is not a luxury, but a necessity. Necessity fuels our pursuits, empowers our endeavors, and inspires us to create a life that resonates with vitality, joy, and the richness of wellbeing. When our health is treated as a treasure, we are then crafting a legacy of positivity, inspiration, and the true fulfilment of a well-lived life.

Necessity fuels our pursuits, empowers our endeavors, and inspires us to create a life that resonates with vitality, joy, and the richness of wellbeing. When our health is treated as a treasure, we are then crafting a
Legacy of positivity, inspiration, and the true fulfilment of a life well-lived.

Journey's Guide

Creativity Time

All over this page, draw symbols, write words, cut and paste pictures from magazines that represent what 'Health' looks like, and feels life for you, and what it could look like and feel like for you.

CHAPTER FIFTEEN

APPRECIATE

'Appreciation can make a day, even change a life.

Your willingness to put it all into words is all that is necessary.'

by Margaret Cousins

Several years ago, my mom and I went to visit my niece in the San Diego area. She was in college at the time, and we stayed at a local hotel while we were in the area. It was a beautiful day, and I wanted to go swimming before meeting up with my niece for dinner. So, my mom and I headed to the pool. When we got to the pool, there was another gentleman taking advantage of the great weather and beautiful pool. As I got into the pool, I greeted him, then I began to swim around him, giving him plenty of room to do his workout. When he was done, he got out of the pool and sat in one of the chairs. I asked him if he was having a good day. This is where I learned one of the most valuable lessons of the transformative power of appreciation, as he replied to my question with; it's a beautiful day in a beautiful place making it a very good day indeed for me.'

From there we did a bit of small talk and then he asked me if the woman I came to the pool with sitting on the opposite side of the pool was my mother. I let him know it was and told him we were in the area visiting my niece. He told me how nice it was to have my mom with me on this visit. He then asked me a question I had never been asked before, "do you appreciate your mom?" I told him that I appreciated her very much, he then asked, 'have you told her that you appreciate her?' Here I am in the pool enjoying the feel of the water as I tread in place enjoying the conversation with this gentleman and find myself moving to the side of the pool to take in what he has just asked me. Had I ever told my mom out loud that I appreciated her? I was sure she knew from everything I did for her and with her; however, I couldn't recall 1 time that I said those exact words.

My mom heard him from across the pool ask me that question, she replied she knew that I did appreciate her. He then asked her, "has she ever told you that she appreciates you?" To which my mom replied that I had told her I loved her. He then looked at me and told me a story about him and his mother, how he loved and adored his mom. They spent a lot of time together and he loved to help her in any way he could.

She unexpectantly passed away and one of the things he realized after she had passed away was the fact that he had never told his mom how much he appreciated her. I could then see the tears begin to form in his eyes. It was after her passing that he really began to think about all she had sacrificed for him to give him the best life possible. He went on to tell me some of the sweet memories he had of his mother and some of the things she had done for him growing up. Before I knew it, it was time for me to get out of the pool and get ready to meet up with my niece. I thanked him for the wonderful conversation and wished him well. The last thing he said to me was 'Be sure to tell your mom as often as you can that you appreciate her! I thanked him, walked over to my mom, and told her, "I appreciate you'. My mom in turn told me she appreciated me as well.

From that time until this present day, in cards I give to my mom, I not only tell her that I love her, I also let her know that I appreciate her. To this day I have also made it a habit to tell her I appreciate her. When we know better, we do better. Showing, telling, and writing to others with gratitude, kindness and recognition are all different forms of appreciation. The gentleman I met that day reminded me of the transformative power of appreciation. He reminded me of the magic that lies within the act of appreciation. Expressing gratitude and acknowledgment has such a profound impact on unlocking the doors to positivity and inspiration. With that little statement, 'have you told her that you appreciate her?', I began to see into the realm of appreciation and understanding the transformative potential, understanding its ripple effects, and recognizing how a simple act of words can alter the course of a day and shape the trajectory of a life. Wow, talk about God putting me in the right place at the right time.

My parents from a very early age taught me the valuable lesson of appreciation. Whenever I received a gift, I was encouraged to write a thank you note. Even though I had already told that person 'thank you' when they gave the gift to me. My parents taught me that showing appreciation is the act of recognizing the worth, value, and contributions of others, and expressing it with sincerity and warmth. Appreciation is more than a social nicety; it's a powerful tool that bridges gaps, fosters connection, and enriches our relationships with others.

One of the best administrators I ever had the privilege to work with was a master in appreciation. He was not only great at expressing it in person, but he was also excellent when it came to writing notes and placing them in our mailboxes or baking cookies and putting them in a small bag with a note attached or a candy bar. Every time I would receive those verbal words of appreciation or discover one of his notes in my mailbox, it was just like receiving a million dollars. He was validating my work and validating me as a person of worth. It renewed me and rejuvenated me in so many incredible ways. His act of appreciating not only me, but our faculty, staff, and students didn't merely touch the surface for all of us, it transformed our campus and community and the experiences we were able to offer each other and our student body. It lifted our spirits, boosted our self-esteem, and infused us with a sense of purpose and validation.

Just like many of the things I have mentioned so far in this book, the impact of appreciation is like a pebble dropping into a calm pond, its ripples extend far beyond the point of contact. When we express appreciation, we not only brighten someone's day but also create a ripple effect that touches those around them. The energy of gratitude radiates outward, enhancing the atmosphere and inspiring others to embrace a similar attitude of appreciation.

As an activities director and an athletic coach, I made it a point to have my leadership students and athletes write thank you notes to the people who came to support us or help us in whatever way they helped us to make our events possible. It's important to acknowledge others for giving their time, support and sometimes their financial support to help us accomplish a task. In almost every one of these events, those people were giving their time and support freely to us. My leadership students and athletes discovered that those thank you notes of appreciation were the glue that cemented the bonds of the relationships of those who helped us. We were showing that we valued those very special people, they were strengthening the connection between individuals, fostering an environment of trust, respect, and mutual support. When individuals feel valued and acknowledged, they are more likely to contribute their best efforts.

Appreciation can also serve as a catalyst for personal growth and development. When we acknowledge someone's efforts and achievements, we provide them with the affirmation needed to continue their journey of improvement. As they receive appreciation, individuals are motivated to explore new horizons, take challenges, and refine their skills, knowing that their endeavors are recognized and valued. As mentioned before, words hold immense power. The act of putting appreciation into words is a transformative endeavor. It elevates our thoughts into actions that can brighten a day and leave an indelible mark on a life. A simple sentence or a heartfelt note can be a beacon of light that guides someone through moments of doubt and darkness. When we train ourselves to see the blessings in our lives and acknowledge the contributions of others, we shift our focus from what's lacking to what's abundant. This shift in perspective opens the door to a life filled with positivity, contentment, and a deep sense of well-being.

When we create a culture of appreciation, we sow the seeds of kindness and empathy. These seeds take root, grow, and bear fruits in the form of compassionate individuals who carry forward the legacy of acknowledging and valuing others. Appreciation has a domino effect, inspiring acts of goodness and generosity. By embracing appreciation as a way of life, we become catalysts for change. We become more positive, we embrace a life woven with threads of kindness, empathy, and heartfelt recognition. May we remember the magic that resides within our words of appreciation and let us use this magic to make days brighter, to change lives, and to contribute to a world filled with inspiration and positivity.

Journey's Guide

1. Who are three people you need to say in person 'I appreciate you' What do you appreciate about them?

2. Who are three people you would like to write a note of appreciation to? Why do you appreciate them?

3. Where in your life have you been shown appreciation? When you received that appreciation, how did it make you feel? What did it do for your relationship with that person? Did this show of appreciation create a ripple effect for you to want to show appreciation to someone else? Why or why not?

4. Right now, and right here, write a letter of appreciation for yourself. What do you appreciate about yourself, your life, those you surround yourself with. Anything at all that you can acknowledge and validate about yourself, tell yourself. 'Thank You.'

CHAPTER SIXTEEN

POSITIVE

Choose to be optimistic, it feels better.'

By Dalai Lama

In a world that seems to focus more on the negative, I make the choice to focus on the positive. It doesn't mean that I am being naïve. I choose how much news I take in. I choose who I surround myself with, I choose to bring optimism to those I meet. I choose to illuminate a path to positivity. In our life we have both joy and challenges. We hold within us the power to choose our perspective. To paraphrase the Dalai Lama, 'choosing to be optimistic, feels better.' This coming from a man who was exiled from his country and has faced major challenges and obstacles in every area of his life it's unimaginable and yet, he chooses to be optimistic.

Optimism isn't merely a disposition; it's a conscious choice to view life through a lens of hope and positivity. It's the belief that challenges are opportunities in disguise, setbacks are steppingstones, and difficulties are gateways to growth. Optimism isn't about denying the existence of hardships; it's about acknowledging them while holding onto the belief that brighter days are within our reach. Our perspective is a powerful instrument that shapes our reality. When we choose optimism, we redirect our focus from problems to solutions, from obstacles to opportunities. When we do this, we illuminate our life's path with the light of possibility. Just as I did when I shared my story of my motorhome burning.

Positivity can serve as a catalyst that can propel us forward on our life's journey. For this pathfinder, I have found that this positivity has taught me about the resilience and fortitude I have. It has given me an inner strength that empowers me to navigate the storms of life with grace. Adversities may still arise, but my response is marked with courage and the belief that I possess the resources to overcome. As mentioned earlier, our choices, including the choice to be optimistic, ripple outward. It not only influences our life experiences but also the lives of those around us. Positivity is contagious, spreading like a warm embrace.

When we radiate optimism, we also create a domino effect like we did with appreciation. We can uplift those who cross our path and can begin a chain reaction of encouragement and hope. When I was teaching, one of the signs I had on the wall in the front of my classroom said, 'Attitudes are contagious, is yours worth catching'? (author unknown) There were many days I needed to be reminded of that saying more than my students. I knew as they entered my classroom, if my attitude was not a good one, that is exactly what I would be getting back from them as well and vice versa.

I encourage you right now to say that quote out loud 'Attitudes are contagious, is yours worth catching' Is it? Life is a journey of ebbs and flows, where challenges often cross over with triumphs. Optimism doesn't shield us from difficulties, instead it equips us with the resilience needed to weather the storms. It's during the most trying times that our choice to be optimistic becomes a lifeline, allowing us to hold onto hope and navigate through the darkness with determination. The choice to be optimistic nurtures a growth-oriented mindset. Rather than viewing failures as endpoints, optimism transforms them into steppingstones towards progress. It encourages us to extract lessons from each experience, understanding that even in the face of adversity, there is an opportunity for growth and refinement.

All the years that I was an athletic coach for tennis, basketball, and softball, my teams never lost. What we did have were 'temporary setbacks.' My athletes weren't 'losers.' It was all about a change of perspective. We were changing the narrative. They were learning that when we had those 'temporary setbacks', it was an opportunity for growth and refinement for our next game.

Optimism isn't confined to personal well-being. It also extends to our creativity. When we view challenges through the lens of optimism, our minds can explore unconventional solutions, envision new possibilities, and discover pathways that might have remained hidden in the shadows of negativity. Positivity can help us with thinking outside the box. Helping us to navigate uncharted territory with courage and ingenuity. Optimism and positivity affect our well-being.

Studies have shown that optimism is linked to lower levels of stress, improved mental health, enhanced immune function, and a longer lifespan. When we choose positivity, we nurture our physical, emotional, and mental health, nurturing us from the inside out. When we feel good about ourselves, our relationships with others thrive. By approaching interactions with others with an optimistic outlook, we open the lines of communication, empathy, and mutual support. Positivity in our connections deepens our bonds, creating a network of encouragement that can help us during challenging times and celebrate during our moments of triumph.

The choice to be optimistic has the power to inspire hope, not only within us but also within the world at large. Our journey towards positivity becomes a testament to the human spirit's capacity to overcome, adapt and evolve. As we radiate optimism, we become beacons of hope, inspiring others to choose optimism in their own lives. Choosing to embark on a journey towards optimism isn't a passive one. It's an active commitment to cultivate a mindset that seeks the light within even the darkest moments. Positivity isn't a naïve rosy view of life. It is taking a stance of empowerment that fuels us forward towards growth, resilience, and the belief in the beauty of possibilities. What do you say we embrace this choice? As we do, let us be witnesses to how our lives can vibrate with optimism and assist us to a well-lived life. It's all a part of living your best *Dash*.

Journey's Guide

Creativity Time

Get out your markers, crayons, colored pencils, or whatever writing device you choose. You are going to write down (however you like on this page) all the words you can think of that convey positivity, optimism, joy, and happiness. Make it colorful, draw the words in different styles and assorted sizes. The idea is to bring a smile to your face as you write these words and to help you feel more positive and optimistic each time you see this page.

CHAPTER SEVENTEEN

PLAYFUL

*We don't stop playing because we grow old;
we grow old because we stop playing.'*

by George Bernard Shaw

Now is the time to embrace the timeless joy of play. It really is what helps to keep us younger. A couple of years ago, I had the opportunity and great pleasure of hearing the incredible motivational speaker Les Brown give a talk. One of the things he said that day that was a great eye-opening moment for me was the following.

'It has been said; most people die at age 25 and don't get buried until they are 65. Make an effort to live your life to the fullest.'

Wow, I had to immediately write that statement down and sit with that statement for a time. How many of you can think of someone you know or knew that fits that statement? For some strange and sad reason, there seems to be a point when many people forget the importance of laughter, creativity, and using their imagination. It seems that play often becomes the casualty of the passage of time. The above quote by George Bernard

Shaw serves as a reminder to me that play isn't just a frivolous pastime. When we understand the significance of play, we then understand its transformative power and recognize how it keeps our spirit and soul young forever. When we begin to realize that play is a state of being that can transcend the boundaries of age, we cannot then not be confined to a specific activity or setting. Play allows us to have an attitude that infuses life with joy and spontaneity. When we engage in play, we surrender to the moment, we embrace the sheer pleasure of the experience without worrying about outcomes or judgments. Play is where our inner child thrives, it's where our imagination takes flight and the burdens of adulthood momentarily fade away.

Play can serve as a type of Fountain of Youth for us. Play can give us vibrant energy, boundless curiosity, and fearless exploration. When we choose not to play, that is when we close the door to these qualities and allow the rigidity of adulthood to overshadow the joy and spontaneity of our inner child. When we tap into that childlike wonder, we tap into a world of creativity and imagination. It allows us to embrace life with renewed wonder and enthusiasm. The act of play can ignite the flame of joy within us and remind us that age is nothing, but a number and the magic of life is ours to embrace.

Play is one of those things that can affect every area of our life. Many people think it is only when we are looking for things to do during our leisure time. In our professional lives, play can bring about innovation, spark ingenuity, and break up the monotony of our usual routines. In our personal lives, play has a way of deepening connections with others, it enhances communication and adds light-hearted energy in our interactions with others. Play enriches our lives by adding vibrancy, depth, and even a touch of whimsy. When we incorporate play into our personal and professional lives, our overall health and well-being can also improve.

By engaging in playful activities, we are releasing endorphins, which happen to be the body's natural 'feel good' chemicals, which have been shown to reduce stress, boost mood, and enhance cognitive function. Play also promotes physical activity, contributing to improved cardiovascular health and enhanced flexibility. Play is a holistic remedy that renews our body, mind, and spirit. As adults, we tend to put self-imposed limitations on ourselves. Our inhibitions seem to heighten, and we have fears of judgment.

When we bring play into our lives, it serves as a liberating force that breaks those chains of conformity. When we play, we don't restrict our expressions, allowing us to dance, sing, create, and explore without reservation. Play brings us back into the realm of possibilities. When we approach life's challenges with a playful spirit, we open ourselves to new solutions and new perspectives. Play encourages us to view problems as puzzles to be solved, rather than obstacles to be overcome. Many of the top grossing corporations around the world find that when they introduce and provide time of play in the workplace, creativity brings about ideas that revolutionize their companies, it sparks movements and redefines the boundaries of what is possible.

One of my most favorite things about play is it creates lasting memories. Those tend to be the moments I cherish most often. Those memories always bring a smile to my face and warm my heart. Playing a spontaneous game with family and friends, going on an adventure, creating new art projects, all of which create an unforgettable experience for everyone involved. These memories also remind me of the joy and happiness that make life special. Participating in play is part of 'enjoying the journey'. Play brings a twinkle to our eyes and a skip to our steps.

It puts a smile on our face, and joy in our souls. It's about allowing ourselves to engage in unstructured, imaginative pursuits that awaken our creativity and renew our spirit. Play can be found in our hobbies, engaging in physical activities, or simply finding moments of silliness. May George Bernard Shaw's quote serves as a reminder that the spirit of play is necessary to live our best *Dash*. It's a call to embrace life with childlike enthusiasm, to infuse every moment with laughter, curiosity, and boundless wonder. It's a declaration that life is a playground of possibilities waiting to be explored. So, what do you say we get out there and answer the call to play, to dance, and create. Let's not grow old because we stopped playing, let us embrace the timeless joy of play and forever remain young at heart.

Journey's Guide

1. Think back to when you were a child. What kinds of things did you consider to be 'play'?

2. As an adult, has your view of play changed? Why or why not?

3. What hinders you from being more playful?

4. What kinds of benefits do you see from adding play into your day?

5. Who are the people in your life that bring fun, joy, and happiness into your life?

6. Who are the people you can add fun, joy, and happiness to their lives?

CHAPTER EIGHTEEN

THE POWER OF YES

'Always say 'yes' to the present moment. Say Yes to life and see how life suddenly starts working for you rather than against you.'

by Eckhart Tolle

Did you know that your fist is the same size as your heart? Yep, that's right. When I was taking my anatomy class in college, I learned that fact. Now, some of you right now are wondering, what does that have to do with saying yes? Here is exactly how it fits into this chapter. Because that fact had such an impact on me, I used it as a motivational technique during my thirty years of teaching. I would have my students in my class, or the student body at an assembly or the adults when I was doing professional development presentations take their dominant hand and make a fist with it and then place it upon their heart. I would then tell them about their fist being the size of their heart, and I encouraged them to tap into what were their dreams, desires, ambitions, and goals. I would then have them raise their fist in the air and on the count of three and yell "YES" as loudly as they could, bringing their fist down. It was their declaration to be in the moment, saying yes to life, and saying yes to what they want from life.

When you begin to see the power of saying Yes to life, that is when you begin to embrace life with open arms. That is when you begin to realize all the infinite possibilities. We get so caught up in our hectic lives that we find ourselves regretting things from our past and worry about our future, which means we are disconnected from the present moment. When we start living mindfully, and embrace the power of the present moment, we are then invited into our life's positivity, inspiration, and transformation. The power of Yes needs a shift in perspective. When we say "YES" to the present moment, our dreams, ambitions, and goals, it doesn't mean to merely acknowledge its existence, it involves embracing it. It means letting go of resistance, doubt, and preconceived notions, and stepping into the flow of life with open arms. When we make this shift, that is when the beauty, wonder, and opportunities around us are magnified.

I admit that I am not always very good about embracing 'the Now.' I often find myself residing in the past or projecting into the future. When I find myself doing this, it reminds me of the quote by Eleanor Roosevelt 'Yesterday is history. Tomorrow is a mystery. Today is a gift. That's why we call it The Present; Tomorrow is not guaranteed to any of us.' Why not embrace the now? Take a moment to feel the gentle breeze blowing outside, listen to the laughter, or smell the rich aroma of a freshly bloomed flower. These moments also can amplify our sense of gratitude. Today is a gift. When we say Yes to life, it's a way of forging a partnership with the universe. It's a recognition that life 'isn't a series of hurdles to overcome, but a journey of discovery, growth, and potential. Our challenges are then transformed into opportunities for learning, and our setbacks become steppingstones towards our future. The Yes mindset is grounded in a sense of openness and acceptance.

It's about relinquishing that need for control and surrendering to the beauty of life's unfolding. This doesn't mean we don't plan or prepare for the future, rather, it allows us to infuse our activities with a sense of grace and adaptability. By accepting the "YES" mindset, we navigate life's twists and turns with resilience and optimism and not the weight of resistance. Life is a dance of opportunities that arise in the present moment. The invitation to say "YES" to these opportunities is an invitation to participate fully in this dance. We can leap into the unknown with a heart full of courage. We allow ourselves to tap into the potential opportunities and open the doors that lead to growth, joy, and fulfillment. The act of saying Yes to life doesn't just transform our own experience, it also radiates positivity to those around us. Our energy is contagious, and when we embrace life with enthusiasm and openness, we inspire others to do the same.

There is also a kind of liberation when we let go. When we practice saying Yes, we liberate ourselves from past regrets and future anxieties. It's our declaration that we are no longer bound by the limitations of our past or the uncertainty of tomorrow. By embracing the present, we free ourselves from the weight of regrets and worries.

As we navigate life's journey, we are not passive observers, we are active participants through our intentions, choices, and actions. We are creating our reality through the choices we make. All of this is about creating a life that works for you. Eckhart Tolle's quote is a call to a life that is vibrant, purposeful, and deeply fulfilling. The act of saying yes to the present moment is an act of empowerment, a commitment to living authentically, and a pledge to unlock all the opportunities that life has to offer. By embracing the yes mindset, we shift our relationship with the present and transform it from a moment in time into a wellspring of potential and positivity. Remember the magic that lies in saying "YES"! So, place your fist upon your heart, think of your dreams, desires, ambitions, and goals. Raise your fist in the air, and on the count of three bring your fist down and yell... Yes.

Journey's Guide

1. Write down your dreams, desires, ambitions, and goals.

2. Do you say 'YES' to those dreams, desires, ambitions, and goals? If you do, in what ways do you say yes? If you don't, why not?

3. Are you good about being 'in the moment'? If you are, what does that look like for you? If not, what can you do to be more present?

4. What does Eckhart Tolle's quote say to you about your life?

5. Does Eleanor Roosevelts quote resonate with you?

CHAPTER NINETEEN

PRIORITIZING SELF-CARE AND SELF-LOVE

"It's not selfish to love yourself, take care of yourself and to make happiness a priority. It's necessary.

by Mandy Hale

Since retiring, I have learned many life lessons, I believe the biggest lesson of all is that I have learned and taken to heart is the lesson on self-care and self-love. My entire adult life I was so busy taking care of everyone else in my life that I forgot to take care of me. By the time I decided to retire, I was extremely obese, out of shape, and exhausted mentally, physically, and spiritually.

The first thing I decided once I retired was to gain back my physical, mental, and spiritual strength. Once I started to do that by exercising, eating better, meeting up with family and friends, going on day trips, taking naps, or just resting, crafting, reading for pleasure, and going on extended trips. I began to realize I had granted myself permission to take care of me and did not feel guilty about it. I also realized I had allowed my cup to be emptied so much that I didn't even know where the cup was.

Now I was doing things for myself for the pure joy and pleasure of it, not because I had to. Being a type A personality, I knew when I started all my retirement business ventures, I needed to find a balance between work time and time for enjoyment. I had begun a journey to wholeness and fulfillment and wanted to keep that a priority for this next chapter of my life. I know I am worth it and so are you. Our world and especially in the United States, we often glorify self-sacrifice and endless giving. Manday Hale's quote above is a powerful reminder of the importance of self-care and self-love. So many of us tend to overlook the demands of our daily life. This quote reminds me to reevaluate our understanding of self-care and self-love, and to embrace them not as acts of indulgence, but as vital elements of a life well-lived. When we add self-care and self-love as a priority, we can see that when our overall well-being is being taken care of, we can see the profound impact it will have towards paving a path to a more positive and fulfilling existence. To some, there is often the notion that self-care and self-love is an indulgent pursuit and even labeled as selfish. It's time to shift that type of thinking.

Self-care is not synonymous with self-indulgent. It is a deliberate and conscious practice of nurturing our physical, emotional, and mental well-being. Along with that, self-love is not narcissism. It is an act of recognizing and honoring our own intrinsic worth. When we begin to use these definitions as the foundation of our own self-care and self-love, we can then understand that we must first fill our own cups before we can pour into the cups of others. A couple of years ago, I was attending an online webinar when another woman made the statement, "I don't pour from my cup to others. I pour from my saucer into the cups of others." Wow, that was a major golden nugget of wisdom for me to hear this statement.

It is crucial to prioritize self-care. Imagine a garden where the gardener takes care of every plant, making sure each one receives enough sunlight, water, and nutrients. This is how self-care nurtures the garden of our lives. It's about listening to our bodies, acknowledging our emotions, and addressing our needs. It's carving out time for activities to restore us physically, to set healthy boundaries, and a commitment to our spiritual well-being. When we prioritize self-care, we bring vitality, resilience, and energy that is required in our lives to navigate life's challenges. Next is fueling the flame of self-love: This is the cornerstone upon which our entire self-concept rests. It's about embracing our flaws and imperfections, recognizing our strengths and talents, and treating ourselves with the same kindness and compassion we extend to others. Self-love isn't a destination to be reached. It is an ongoing journey that requires patience, acceptance, and a commitment to growth.

When we cultivate self-love, we create a safe space where we can grow, learn, and evolve. The pursuit of well-being encompasses the physical, emotional, mental, and spiritual dimension of our lives. Self-care and self-love provide the structure for this holistic approach. Let's use a four-legged table as an example, the table will only be stable when all the legs are supported equally. Our well-being is only in balance when all areas of our being are nurtured. When one or more of those areas are being neglected, that leads to an imbalance that affects all areas of our lives. When we prioritize self-care and self-love, we establish a solid foundation for a life full of positivity and fulfillment.

One of the greatest obstacles to embracing self-care and self-love is the guilt that often accompanies these practices. Society's expectations and cultural conditioning have led many to believe that prioritizing ourselves is at odds with being a responsible, caring individual. However, this couldn't be further from the truth. Just as an airplane passenger is instructed to put on their own oxygen mask before assisting others, prioritizing self-care ensures that we're equipped to offer our best selves to those around us.

We need to release guilt and embrace self-care as a necessity. When we take the time for self-care and self-love, we begin to lay the groundwork for healthier relationships with others. When we nurture our own well-being, our positivity, compassion, and vitality enrich our interactions with our family, friends, and co-workers. That is when we begin to model and inspire others to embark on their own journeys of well-being. You will notice that your examples of self-care and self-love will have a ripple effect and will begin to encourage those you interact with to prioritize their own self-care and self-love.

Have you ever heard the statement 'How do you eat an elephant? One bite at a time.' The journey to prioritizing self-care and self-love begins with your first conscious decision to begin. With that first bite you are setting into motion a commitment to treat yourself with the same kindness, respect, and consideration that you extend to others. Start by just setting aside five minutes a day. Take time to enjoy your favorite beverage, get some sun on your face, read your favorite book or magazine. Yes, there will be ups and downs, victories, and setbacks. Keep in mind that each step forward is an act of empowerment and a declaration that our well-being matters, and our happiness is worth pursuing.

The power of self-care and self-love reminds us that prioritizing our own well-being is not a selfish act. It is a necessary foundation for a life that is vibrant, meaningful, and fulfilling. By embracing self-care and self-love, our journey forward in this life is vibrant, meaningful, fulfilling and enriches our relationships with others. Dare to love yourself, care for yourself, and make happiness a priority. Choose a path of empowerment, positivity, and self-discovery. Let it be a journey that leads to living your best *DASH*.

Journey's Guide

1. On this page write down what you are feeling right now. No judgments, just write.

2. Find three self-love affirmations that you would like to repeat to yourself for the next week and write them down here.

3. Over the next week, give yourself 10 minutes before you get out of bed and just lie there. Be in the moment and enjoy this time. After a couple of days doing this, write down how this time has felt to you.

4. Do you practice one or more of these self-care, self-love activities: Meditation, Visualization, Yoga and Stretching, or Breathing techniques? If so, which ones do you practice and if not, research each one and see if one or more of them look like something you would like to add into your daily routine.

5. Write a love letter to yourself. Include things you like about yourself, your gifts, talents, things you have accomplished or things that others have complimented you on. What are the things you appreciate about yourself? Whenever you are having a tough time, take out this letter and read it to remind yourself of this self-love.

CHAPTER TWENTY

LET GO AND LET GOD

Nurturing our Spiritual Health and Wellbeing

Let go and let God is not about being stagnant. It's about trusting God in the midst of the situation and moving forward in faith."

by Melissa Tumino

Over my lifetime the following words continued to repeat in my brain, Let Go and Let God. You may refer to it as your higher power, spirit, love, infinite intelligence, just to name a few. Sounds so simple, doesn't it? Is it really that simple, could it be that simple? I guess it all depends on your belief system. Each morning, I begin my day with a 30-to-60-minute devotional time and end my day with a 15-to-30-minute devotional time. Up until a couple of years ago I basically created my own type of devotional sessions. It included meditation, breathing exercises, read the Bible in a year, just to name a few. At the beginning of 2023, my friend Christa asked me if I'd be interested in getting a book that the board of her church were encouraged to read over the next year called Core 52. Each of the 52 weeks in this year has a chapter with a particular theme for the week that is related to different areas of the Bible.

An example of one of the week's messages was 'The Golden Rule'; Do unto others as you would have them do unto you. Once again, it sounds simple, doesn't it, but is it, could it be? I believe it comes down to some of the following things, beliefs, hope, faith, and trust. One of the evening devotionals I was reading ended with the following sentence: Let your uniqueness define your path of life. When your business is called "Pathways with Patti", you tend to key into how the word 'Path' is being used. So, of course this sentence stood out to me in so many ways. Part of my own uniqueness goes back to my opening statement: finding myself saying (Let Go and Let God). Do I really do that? To be honest, some days it is easier than others. Since retiring, those four simple words have become a strong mantra for me. After a lifetime of living out my passion and purpose as an educator, I had no clue what I was going to do for the rest of my life. For me, this is where I needed to really test my own belief system. Did I have hope for my future? How strong was my faith? Did I really trust that my higher power, known as God, would guide me to create a new path for my life and to discover my uniqueness to help others and create a legacy, I could be proud of.

To stay true to myself and my uniqueness, letting go and letting God is exactly what I want and need to do to accomplish the things I need to do with my life. This also means to me that by letting go, I allow God to bring those special people into my life to help me by teaching me how to build upon my uniqueness to motivate and inspire others. There is a profound significance of nurturing our spiritual health for a life filled with joy and inner peace. I know that my spiritual journey is something that ignites my soul with meaning and purpose. At the core of our human existence is the quest for connection. Connection with ourselves, with others, and with the universe at large. Our spiritual health is how we make that connection and offers us a sense of belonging and wholeness. When we cultivate a deep awareness of our inner being, we embark on a transformative journey of self-discovery, uncovering an unlimited reservoir of wisdom, compassion and love that resides inside of us.

In today's world, we can easily get caught up in keeping up with the Jones' when it comes to external validation and material gain. However, we usually find that true fulfillment eludes us until we turn inward and nurture our spiritual health. When we practice things such as meditation, prayer, or mindfulness techniques, we tap into a sacred space where we can retreat to replenish our spirits and find solace amidst life's storms. Our spiritual health empowers us to get through life's twists and turns with grace and resilience. In times of trouble, it is our spiritual foundation that sustains us by giving us strength and courage to persevere in the face of challenges. It is through those moments of introspection and reflection that we gain invaluable insights into the deeper meaning behind our experiences, finding wisdom amid uncertainty and clarity among the chaos. Nurturing our spiritual health enriches our relationships with others, fosters deeper connections, builts on empathy, understanding and unconditional love. Our spiritual well-being enables us to go beyond the barriers of ego and judgment, creating a sense of unity and interconnectedness with all we engage with.

Our spiritual health helps us to embrace a much wider perspective on the interconnectedness of our world. The sacredness of all life, nature and being inspired to live in harmony with it all. It is then that we become stewards of the earth and feel a responsibility to preserve it for future generations. For me, my spiritual health has helped me to become clearer about my unique gifts and talents and learn how to use them for the greater good of my community. I pray that I have many more years on this planet to do as much good as possible. With that said, if God were to call me home today, I can honestly say 'it's been a wonderful life'.

The people I have been blessed to have in my life both personally and professionally have been incredible. The things I have learned and continue to learn from them and with them have and continue to be priceless. The opportunities they help me to discover, restore my faith in my future endeavors and keep me moving forward. Whatever your spiritual beliefs and faith, let your uniqueness define your path of life.

Remember to nurture your spiritual health and you will find yourself on an incredible transformative journey of self-discovery, connection, and purpose. This is the journey that will lead you closer to your true self. Also remember that when those special someone's or spiritual figures come into your life, either for a season of time or a lifetime, let go and let them help you on your life's journey. You'll be glad you did.

Journey's Guide

1. What does spiritual well-being mean to you?

2. Do you have a spiritual "devotional" practice in place (journal writing, readings, meditation, mindfulness)? Why or why not?

3. What time of the day would be or is best for you? How long is beneficial for you?

CHAPTER TWENTY-ONE

WHAT DOES D.A.S.H MEAN?

"There are two dates on every tombstone. There's a birth date and there is a date of death, and every human being is guaranteed those two dates. But that little dash that lies between those two numbers is what defines our lives.
So, make your dash count. Live. Really live."
wherehopegrowsmovie.com

PART TWO – D.A.S.H.

Daring to Achieve a Successful and Happy Life

Are you living your best life? Let's take it one step further. Are you living your best DASH? For many of you right now, I'm sure you might be thinking about the *Dash* for Cash, the 50–yard dash, or the dash on a keyboard. What's similar with each of these dashes? They all have a beginning and, at some point, an end. However, if you take a closer look at that dash mark on your keyboard; you type it, print it, and put that dash mark under a microscope, it isn't so short. You can see how much longer the line can be. Now, see that dash mark as your life's timeline from birth to death this is Your *Dash*. Are you Daring to Achieve a Successful and Happy life?

When you go to a cemetery and look at someone's headstone, you will see a date of birth, a dash, and date of death. That dash represents that person's time here on earth. If you knew that person, that dash would tell you the story of their life. What does it say to you about how they lived their life and the legacy they left behind? Were they someone who lived a life of regrets, goals not met, or relationships not nurtured? Or was it a life that took advantage of each moment and made their part of the world better than they found it? What will your dash and legacy represent to others?

That Dash is your life story. It's your wishes, goals, and accomplishments that you began to have as a child. What did you want to be when you grew up? Of course, as we get older, the wishes, goals, and ideas about what we want to accomplish in this life change over time. The things we learn and the relationships we build with other people all have an impact on our lives. Some of us kept some or all those goals that we set as children, like I did. Others found that what they wanted to be when they grew up continued to change as they got older. Neither of these ways are right or wrong. It's about the journey and how we deal with each part of that adventure with ourselves and those around us. So, what will be your legacy? It's never too late to create a legacy you can be proud of.

Life is short; we need to make the most of our dash. What do you want your legacy to be when you are no longer here? What words will be spoken about you when people see your dash? You get to choose, how about right now you redefine what it means to be retired, getting ready to retire, being an empty nester, or someone who has lost their passion and purpose for their current career? How about retiring from what you DON'T love and not retiring from life? An amazing thing about our dash and our legacy, it can continue to live on through our family, friends, charities, and foundations. Think of your legacy as a seed. As you interact with others, you are planting seeds of wisdom, knowledge, and experiences. Those seeds will continue to grow and thrive with those whose lives you touched during your lifetime. How cool is that? I do my best to Live my Best Dash each day, I must admit that some days are easier than others.

Part Two

I will be breaking Down the D.A.S.H. To do that, however, I need to start at the beginning. The following poem by Linda Ellis is a great place to start about the meaning behind the *DASH*:

The Dash
by Linda Ellis

I read of a man who stood to speak
at the funeral of a friend
He referred to the dates on the tombstone
from the beginning to the end.

He noted that first came the date of birth
and spoke the following date with tears,
but he said what mattered most of all
was the dash between those years.

For that dash represents all the time
that they spent alive on earth.
And now only those who loved them
know what that little line is worth.

For it matters not, how much we own --
the cars, the house, the cash.
What matters is how we live and love.

and how we spend our dash.

So, think about this long and hard.
Are there things you'd like to change?
For you never know how much time is left
that can still be rearranged.

If we could just slow down enough
to consider what's true and real,
and always try to understand
the way other people feel.

And be less quick to anger
and show appreciation more,
and love the people in our lives
like we've never loved before.

If we treat each other with respect
and more often wear a smile,
remembering this special dash
might only last a little while.

So, when your eulogy is being read
with your life's actions to rehash,
would you be proud of the things they say
about how you spent your dash?

Now, take a moment to read that last paragraph once more. Go ahead, read it. Now, let's break down the D.A.S.H. As a Certified Life-Cycle Celebrant (Wedding & Funeral Officiant), when I am asked to officiate a funeral service, I create a Celebration of Life service, I want to highlight how that person lived their best dash, As Linda Ellis says in her final paragraph. 'So, when your eulogy is being read with your life's actions to rehash, would you be proud of the things they say about how you spent your dash. Your life matters, Be Daring to Achieve a Successful and Happy life because Life's an Adventure, and I feel that everyone should, 'Enjoy their journey.'

Journey's Guide

Draw a tombstone below. Write your full name, below that, your date of birth, draw a dash and todays date of your death. Below the dates, write your favorite quote, saying or poem. Once you have filled in the tombstone, take a moment to look at your dash. How do you feel about the life you have lived?

1. On a separate piece of paper, draw two dash marks. On the first Dash, at the far-left end of the dash, write your date of birth. At the right end of the dash, leave it blank. Starting from your birth, on the dash place marks along the dash that represents milestone events in your life that stand out for you. Below that mark, write a word that describes that event. Do this until you reach the end of the first dash.

2. On the second dash, this starts where you are today until the end of your life. Above the dash mark, place symbols to mark your dreams/goals for your future. Write a word above that symbol to describe that dreams and goal.

3. How do you feel now about how you have lived your *Dash*.

CHAPTER TWENTY-TWO

DARING

"Life is either a daring adventure or nothing at all."
by Helen Keller

Let's break down the word Dash, and you will see how you can make a difference with your life and legacy by Daring to Achieve a Successful and Happy life!

D = Daring: Are you daring to dream and act on what you really want for your life? Are you daring to take the steps needed to make those dreams a reality? Are you daring to live your best life? Are you daring to believe that you deserve to live your best life?

"No crime is so great as daring to excel."
by Winston Churchill

When we look at our lives and the many journeys the paths of life have taken us on, I am sure we can all think about and remember certain points where the journey changed and had a profound effect on our lives. That can have either a negative or positive effect. Some of those events that can take place include, but are not limited to, the illness or death of a loved one, losing a job, a global pandemic, getting a new job, moving to a new location, getting a promotion, getting married, having children, etc. You can decide which of those are negative and which are positive. When these major events take place, this is where we have the choice to be daring with our future and how it will ultimately become a part of our legacy. When we dare to change the trajectory of our life goals and plans, we are making the choice to shake it up and take a leap of faith. Is it scary and frightening? You bet it is; we won't realize it when it seems we are at our darkest moments, but that is when the magic of a new beginning can take place.

We can look at our Dash as a roadmap to embracing a life of incredible dreams, unwavering belief, and profound legacy. Dare to dream, dare to believe, and dare to achieve. Are you daring to dream, allowing your imagination to stretch its wings and soar? Are you daring to take steps towards manifesting those dreams into reality?

In a world filled with opportunities, being daring means grasping the boldness to live your best life, embracing your potential, and believing that you deserve every ounce of happiness and success.

When looking at the quote by Winston Churchill, his words remind us that daring to excel is an act of rebellion against mediocrity. It's about breaking free from the confines of comfort zones and stepping out. When you dare to surpass your own limitations, you embark on a journey of self-discovery, growth, and loads of potential. To dare to excel is to shatter the barriers that limit your progress and unlock the doors to your greatest achievements, we all can be daring with our futures. By refusing to let our circumstances define our path, we can reshape our future goals by the way we look at the events in our lives as positive or negative.

These challenges hold the potential for new beginnings. We are ultimately the authors of our book of life, and we are the ones writing the narrative that is authentically ours. Are you daring to embrace change? To do that, it requires a daring spirit, a willingness to leave the comfort of the familiar and venture into the realm of the unknown. The fear and uncertainty that often accompany change are natural, but they pale in comparison to the exhilaration of embracing new possibilities. When you dare to welcome change, you begin to cultivate the seeds of growth and resilience. You begin to acknowledge that every moment, in the darkest ones, holds the promise of a new start, a new chapter, and a daring adventure waiting to unfold.

Dare to believe in yourself, this belief is a lifeline that fuels your journey, it guides you through the rough patches on your path of life. Believe in your capacity to act, to go beyond your challenges, and to live life boldly. When life's uncertainties seem to be getting the best of you, let your self-belief serve as your compass, pointing you towards your goals and aspirations with great determination.

Dare to create a legacy you can be proud of, your legacy is all your life experiences, choices and actions you have lived throughout your life's journey. Every daring step you take, every dream you pursue becomes a part of your legacy. By daring to make a difference, you create a narrative that will be passed on to future generations. Your legacy isn't just about the marks you leave on the world; it's a testament to the courage and resilience that define your life and time here on earth.

Dare to live boldly. Step onto the stage of life and declare that you refuse to be confined by fear and doubt. Embrace every experience, whether it be a triumph or setback, as a chapter in your daring adventure. Let your story be one of perseverance, resilience, and positivity. Remember that the terrain we travel is ever-changing, and you possess the power to travel this road with audacity and courage,

As you embrace the Daring adventure of life, remember that you are the author of your journey. Each step you take becomes a part of your legacy. Through daring dreams, unwavering belief, and audacious action, you unleash the potential to achieve greatness and inspire others to do the same. The journey may be challenging, but it's within the daring moments that the magic of transformation takes place. Dare to believe in yourself, dare to believe in acting, and dare to believe in living boldly.

Journey's Guide

1. How are you daring to dream?

2. How are you daring to believe in what you want for your life moving forward?

3. How are you daring to achieve a life of living boldly?

4. What needs to be done in your life to be daring to make all the above happen? Is there anything holding you back? If so, what is it and what can you do to change it?

CHAPTER TWENTY-THREE

ACHIEVE

'If my mind can conceive it, and my heart can believe it, I know I can achieve it.'

by Jesse Jackson

A = Achieve: What do you wish to achieve during your life? What would it mean to you to achieve something you have desired? What would achievement look like and what would it feel like to you? Keep your dreams alive. Understanding that to achieve anything requires faith and belief in yourself, vision, hard work, determination, and dedication. Remember all things are possible for those who believe.'

By Gail Devers

Do you have a master life plan, a list of wants or desires for your life? Are you goal setting and bringing those goals to life by writing them down on a piece of paper, or perhaps on a vision board that includes pictures and symbols, and placing that list where they are visible? Those are things that can help you make your dreams achievable. Do you think it's too late in your life to set goals? If your response is yes, is it because of your age, your life circumstances, you just don't believe it to be worth your time, or you don't think goal setting really makes a difference? If any of those ideas are true for you, that type of thinking could keep you from living your best 'Dash'.

For those of you who know it's never too late to set some goals for your life, you are absolutely correct, and you deserve a high five, Just like in the song, 'Don't Stop Believing' by Journey, I'd like to add, 'Never Stop Dreaming' because that leads you to achieving your goals. DO NOT let others 'Yuck your Wows!" If you can dream it and believe it, then you can achieve it. It is about unleashing the power within. It's the journey from dream to achievement. The seeds of achievement are a part of the fertile ground of our thoughts and beliefs. This is where the realm of possibility has the power and potential to transform our dreams into reality and our aspirations into accomplishments.

When we embrace these steps, that is exactly what we need to move us towards our desired objectives. It's about our personal ambitions. To achieve is to strive, to put forth the effort, skill, and courage to pursue a desired outcome. It is a testament to our resilience, our capacity to surmount challenges in our life and our unwavering belief in our potential. We must envision the realization of our goals. In our journey from dream to achievement, faith and self-belief become the cornerstone of our transformation.

We need to nurture those dreams and not let doubt cloud our judgement. Our faith is what fuels our determination, it drives us to work tirelessly and fortifies us to resolve and overcome obstacles. First, we need to create a blueprint for our success. Once you have created that master life plan of your desires and aspirations, it is then time to have a clear vision that encompasses your hopes, dreams, and goals. This master plan isn't something you write on a piece of paper and place it in a folder that goes into your desk. It needs to be a living document that you see daily that shows you your journey ahead. You are etching onto paper or visualizing on a vision board filled with images that resonate with your aspirations. Creating this is an act of externalizing your goals which magnifies their significance, making them tangible reminders of the journey you're embarking upon.

Is it ever too late to set goals, to reach new horizons and stretch the boundaries of what is possible? No, do not let age, circumstances, or skepticism hinder you from pursuing your dreams. If your heart beats with the rhythm of ambition, if your thoughts are teeming with possibilities, you have the capacity to redefine your journey. The journey of achievement isn't confined to a specific timeline. If that were the case, when I retired from teaching, I would have been doing nothing for the past eight years. Instead, I have reinvented my life by going back to school, going to workshops, and webinars. I have become a life-cycle celebrant, started my own business. I am also a speaker, life coach, podcaster, travel agent and author. And I can tell you right now, that list of achievements will continue to grow until my last breath,

Never stop dreaming, our dreams are the compass that guides us towards our goals. To dare to dream, to embrace possibility with open arms, is to embark on a journey that transcends limitations and propels us towards our ultimate potential, Believe, Achieve, Repeat, Believe in yourself and your dreams. External voices, doubt, and negativity can cast shadows on our aspirations. It is essential to shield our dreams from such influences. Embrace the mantra: "If you can dream it and believe it, then you can achieve it." Embrace your dreams as the north star guiding your endeavors. With every accomplishment, your belief in yourself gains momentum, creating a cycle of belief, achievement, and renewed aspirations.

In the grand scheme of life, your achievements are composed of your thoughts, your beliefs, and your actions. Remember how strong you are, remember the potency of your potential. Align your mind's vision with your heart's unwavering belief and move forward on a journey that defies limitations and transcends expectations, from crafting your master life plan to defying age and circumstances.

Remember, every stride you take in the pursuit of your dreams is a testament to your courage and commitment. Cast aside your doubts, embrace the possibilities and let the mantra 'If my mind can conceive it, and my heart can believe it, I know I can achieve it' guide you towards a life of boundless potential, unwavering belief, and inspiring accomplishments. Go get 'em tiger.

Journey's Guide

1. Looking back on your DASH timeline, from now until your final breath, what are three things that you are wanting to achieve?

2. Have you ever written your goals down or created a vision board? Why or why not?

3. What are the steps needed to make those dreams and aspirations a reality?

4. What does it mean for you to achieve a goal?

5. Who are the people who can assist you with achieving your goals? What programs or supplies are needed to achieve your goals?

CHAPTER TWENTY-FOUR

SUCCESSFUL

'Nothing is impossible, the word itself says 'I'm possible,'
By Audrey Hepburn

S = Successful. What does it mean to be successful to you? What would you need to be daring to achieve to be successful?

'Action is the foundational key to all success.'
by Pablo Picasso

Make it a great day or not, the choice is yours, it's easy to blame others and the world for your current life situations. We need to take ownership of our own lives. Stop comparing yourself to others and what you believe to be their success. Put your time and effort toward creating a life that works for you and your brand of what being successful is all about. Some define success as making lots of money. Others believe it is their status at work, home, and/or family. What is your idea of being successful? It's easy to get caught up in the 'rat race' of life, constantly feeling the need to 'compete' and win to be successful.

This is where being thankful and grateful has redefined my thinking about what success looks, feels, and sounds like. I stopped making New Year's resolutions many years ago. I allowed success or failure to those resolutions to determine my way of thinking and feeling (making it a great day or not). In January of 2022 I tried something new for my life. I set a word of intention for the entire year. The word I chose: Gratitude, every Thursday for the entire year, I sent out a 'Thankful Thursday Text' to 22 family members and friends. I posed a different question each week about an area of their life they were 'thankful' and 'grateful' for. I also included my answer to the question. The responses I received from everyone each week reminded me of the many things there were to be grateful for beyond what I had considered. As the year went by, I became more thankful for the simple things in my life, and I began to realize I was more successful than I had thought. What a beautiful life lesson.

Within the realm of success lies a realm of possibility waiting to be unlocked. Success is not merely the accumulation of accolades or material gains, it's a personal journey of growth, fulfillment, and purpose. The path to success is unique to everyone. It's part of your aspirations and goals that resonate with your deepest passions. What defines success for you? What daring feats must you conquer to claim your personal victory? Remember that success isn't a fixed destination, but an evolving journey marked by accomplishments that align with your values and aspirations. To forge the path of success, action is the catalyst that propels dreams into reality. It's easy to get ourselves into a mental and negative self-talk trap of what ifs and uncertainties. It's in our moving forward with action that the seeds of accomplishment take root. Action is the bridge that connects dreams with their realization. Every small step, every decision to move forward, contributes to your road to success. By embracing action, you create a wide array of possibilities for your success.

Our lives are made up of many daily choices. Each of those daily choices creates a different experience. It's easy to blame others or circumstances for our life's challenges, but true empowerment lies in taking ownership of your journey. Your response to situations, your outlook on life and the actions you take are all within your control. Embrace the power to shape your days and your destiny with the choices you make. Redefine success through gratitude. We are often preoccupied with comparisons and societal expectations by the television we watch or the social media we consume on almost a daily basis. It is crucial to define success on your terms. There are some days that my definition of success was just getting out of bed; being grateful for having a nice bed to sleep in and a comfy pillow to place my head upon. It's important to release the burden of measuring your achievements against others. 'Let your own unique journey be the compass that guides you. Success isn't about outpacing others, it's about progressing at your pace and celebrating each milestone, no matter how small it may seem. Cultivate an attitude of gratitude, for it's in the practice of acknowledging the blessings that surround you that you unlock a profound shift in perspective.

The journey to success is a journey of thankfulness and abundance. When we adopt a spirit of thankfulness, it has a way of reshaping our narrative, it opens our eyes to the abundance that surrounds our life. Gratitude and expressions of thankfulness have a ripple effect to not only change how you view success but can expand that awareness to others when they see the success you have already achieved. When we take the time to be thankful daily, you begin to realize that success isn't solely defined by grand accomplishments, but also in our everyday moments, small joys, cherished connections, and the moments that remind you of your abundant life. As you traverse the ever-evolving landscape of your aspirations, let your journey be a testament to the realm of possibility that unfolds when you believe in your potential.

Align your thoughts, words, and actions with your aspirations, and watch as you begin to succeed one intentional step at a time. Define success on your own terms and remember that it's not a destination but a journey marked by personal victories. Through the choices you make and the actions you take, embrace the transformative power of action, for it's the key that unlocks the doors of possibility. You are capable of achieving greatness, with gratitude as your compass and action as your guide. Journey forth into a life where success is not an endpoint but an ever-unfolding story of possibility and potential. 'You are Successful.'

Journey's Guide

Creative Time

Using a multitude of colored pens, pencils, crayons, and markers, fill up this page with words, symbols and drawings that represent success and for what you are grateful.

CHAPTER TWENTY-FIVE

HAPPY

"Happiness is a choice, and today I choose to be happy."

A little Dose of Happy

H = Happy: Are you H-A-P-P-Y? What would it take to make you happy? What would it take for you to bring happiness into the lives of those around you? When you have been daring to achieve success, that will bring about happiness in your life,

"Happiness is when what you think, what you say, and what you do are in harmony."
by Mahatma Gandhi

Too many times, we look to others to make us happy. We look to events, family, and friends, just to name a few, to make us happy. We begin to believe that others can and will make us happy. And they can to a certain extent. But to really become happy, we need to search inside ourselves for the things that bring us joy and truly make us happy. What are you passionate about? Reading a book? Working on a craft project, spending time with special people or helping others? Are you making it a priority to do things that bring you joy? I'm not saying you must be happy all the time. What I'm saying is that you should not just rely on others for your happiness. Of course, you want and need others to be a part of that happiness. I just don't want that to be your only source of achieving happiness. I challenge you every day for the next week to, at some point in your day, look into a mirror and say, 'I Am Happy.'

It comes down to embracing the abundance of joy and making it a proactive pursuit of happiness. Happiness has the power to uplift and transform your life's emotions. Happiness is not a fleeting gift brought about by chance; it is a choice, a conscious decision that can reshape our reality. I know you may be thinking about the notion that happiness may be summoned through a mere choice, and it might sound oversimplified. It's about making a declaration of empowerment; it's like that garden we have talked about in past chapters. When we tend that garden, we are nurturing the seeds of positivity and joy even amidst the harshest storms.

While human experience encompasses a spectrum of feelings, it's your prerogative to choose which feelings you choose to feel. All your feelings when blended create layers of emotions that create your reality. Happiness will emerge as a beacon of hope that can and will illuminate even the gloomiest corners of your existence. This choice to be happy is not a passive surrender to circumstances, but an active engagement with life.

It's an understanding that happiness is not solely dependent on external validation or the fulfillment of every desire. Happiness is something built from within, it is nurtured by gratitude for the present moment and a deep-rooted belief in your ability to navigate life's twists and turns. Choosing happiness is not a denial of pain or life's challenges; it's a conscious decision to acknowledge them while refusing to let them define your narrative. It's a recognition that setbacks are steppingstones, and difficulties are opportunities for growth. When you choose happiness, you embrace the power to transform adversity into wisdom, disappointment into determination, and pain into resilience.

It's important to understand that choosing happiness is not just a one than done proclamation; it's a practice, a daily commitment to self-care and self-compassion. Using mindfulness techniques is one way that happiness allows you to really absorb the richness of each moment. Embrace gratitude, when you do this, it shifts your focus from what's lacking to the abundance that surrounds you. Engage in acts of kindness, they can create that ripple effect of positivity that extends far beyond your immediate space. When it comes to human connections, your choice to be happy serves as an inspiration, a testament to the incredible spirit that resides in each of us.

When others witness your commitment to joy, they are reminded that they too possess the choice to shape their emotions as well. Your choice becomes a catalyst for a ripple effect as the warmth of your happiness touches the lives of those around you, encouraging them to embark on their own journeys of positivity. The journey to choosing happiness doesn't move forward in a straight line. It's important to grant yourself grace on the days when clouds seem to be blocking the sun, metaphorically speaking.

These moments are not a failure of your choice, but rather an invitation to delve deeper into your emotional toolkit (this book is about helping you achieve, by adding to your emotional toolkit). When these dark days come upon us, seek solace in the embrace of loved one, find comfort in activities that ignite your passion, and remind yourself of the triumphs you've already achieved on your journey toward happiness.

Today, as you stand at the crossroads of time, take a moment to reflect on the power you hold within you. The power to shape your reality, the power to infuse each day with purpose, and the power to choose happiness. We are all fully aware of the limitations the world emphasizes; when you choose happiness, you become a testament to the limitless potential that lies with the human spirit. Your choice to be happy is a testament to your courage, your strength, and your resilience. As you navigate the map of life. Remember that happiness is not a distant shore; it's a treasure that dwells inside of you, waiting to be unearthed through your conscious choice. Let your days be filled with decisions to be joyful and let your life be an inspiration to all who witness the transformative power of embracing happiness as a choice.

When we harmonize with happiness, we can begin to cultivate joy from within us. It's true that people, experiences, and connections can bring moments of happiness into our lives. The laughter shared with loved ones, celebrating achievements, and the warmth of companionship all contribute to our varied emotions. Be careful not to place all your happiness in the hands of external factors. Embark on a journey inward. What are those activities that light up your soul? What pursuits make time seem to stand still? When you engage in these passions, it's like tending to the flame of your own inner happiness. Finding happiness within doesn't mean we negate the importance of relationships and shared experiences. It empowers you to approach these connections from a place of positivity, which radiates energy outward and enhances the experiences we share with others. Your interactions become a harmonious exchange.

Earlier in this chapter, I asked you to look in a mirror and say, "I'm H-A-P-P-Y," Just as I practiced with my students when I was teaching in public education; I won't ask you to do something that I haven't done. Each morning when I get out of bed, when I see myself in the bathroom mirror, I take a second to say those words and make myself smile at myself. No matter what mood I woke up in, this morning ritual puts a smile on my face. I also know that when I do this, it flips an invisible switch in my brain that transforms my thinking from being tired, sore, sad, or a multitude of emotions into an overall emotion of gratitude. For having the opportunity to be alive another day and to make a difference. Give it a try and see how it can not only transform your morning, but your entire day.

May you continue to choose happiness, not as a destination, but as a daily intention. Embrace the power you hold within and remember that the journey to happiness is as much about the process as it is about the destination.

Let the mantra "I'm H-A-P-P-Y" be a gentle reminder that you're the author of your own joy, and your story is one of empowerment, resilience, and positivity. Is that a smile I see on your face?

Journey's Guide

Creative Time

Write down the titles of songs, stories, poems, quotes, and words that make you happy, make you smile. And while your creative juices are flowing, color in the happy face.

CHAPTER TWENTY-SIX

YOUR LIFE MATTERS

"Your life has purpose. Your story is important. Your dreams count. Your voice matters. You were born to make an impact."

by unknown

My first full time teaching job was one of growth on many levels. I was in a brand-new community where I didn't know anyone, and no one knew me. One of the things I was taught in my student teaching classes was to not get close to your students. This concept was a bit strange for me to absorb. By the time I got this full-time job, I had already been coaching high school athletic teams for five years, teaching my athletes what it meant to be part of a team, to look out for and support each other as a team / family. Teaching this and building upon that concept was at the core of my being not only as a coach but as a person. So being taught to keep my students at arm's length and only looking at them as an ID number and not as a person, went against my beliefs of what I had experienced and learned from my teachers and mentors.

That first semester I taught at this new school, I found myself with a particular student named Michael. Michael was a sophomore also new to the area. During Michaels lunch period, he would come out to my class and hang out. It was during this time that I found out that Michael's dad was in prison and his mom was a drug addict. Michael had been brought to the high desert from Los Angeles to live with his aunt and uncle for that school year. He was very upset, depressed, and lonely. In the class that Michael was in there were two students that were wonderful people, Julie and Todd. Through the first quarter, I would make sure to put Michael in groups and teams that these other two students were a part of. Before I knew it, the three of them became great friends.

When the second quarter began, the three of them would visit me before school started each morning and they continued to come out to my class during their lunch period. Keeping these three students as just an ID number was not going to happen. Right after Thanksgiving break, before school started that day, Julie and Todd came to my office to see if I had seen Michael. I informed them that I had not seen him yet. They told me they had gone to his house to pick him up where he told them he was not ready yet and would meet up with them at school. I was out on the tennis courts teaching my fourth period class when one of my administrators walked over saying 'he would cover my class. I was to go to the office to speak to a sheriff officer.' For the life of me, I couldn't think of why an officer would need to talk to me.

This is when I was informed that after Micheal had told Julie and Todd he would see them later at school, he went into his aunt and uncle's camper in the backyard, filled a paper bag with blue spray paint, inhaled it and then shot himself in the head. The next thing I heard the officer saying to me. 'We understand that you were Michael's favorite teacher, is there anything he may have said to you that would lead you to believe he would kill himself?' Still in shock from this devastating news, my mind began to reel through the many conversations Michael, and I had over the past several months. I knew that the first quarter was difficult for him, but since becoming friends with Julie and Todd, I had seen Michael as a teenager who had turned a corner smiling, laughing, and seemed to be enjoying life. For the life of me, as I traced back through my memory, I couldn't think of one thing Michael had said to me that would lead me to believe he would harm himself or anyone else. I let the officer know, I couldn't think of anything. I told him how well he was doing in school and that he had two good friends. The officer wanted to know who those friends were, and he would call them in to talk with them.

He gave me his card and asked me to call him if I could think of anything. The rest of that school day was a blur for me. I received a phone call from one of our counselors that there would be a gathering held for any students or staff that needed to meet in the library after school to talk about Michael and what had happened. It was at this counseling gathering that I saw Julie and Todd. There were no words between the three of us, only one long, big, tight hug. It was at this gathering that I learned the saying 'Suicide is a permanent solution to a temporary problem.' I remember the events of this day, which were now thirty-seven years ago, like it was yesterday. I often think of the man Michael would have been and the life he could have had.

Fast forward to ten years ago, there was a student attending our local junior college who killed himself. He was twenty years old, and our high desert community was crushed even though we didn't know who he was. It was the fact that this young man with so much life and potential didn't think there was any hope for his future. That night after the news broke about this young man, I drove past the college on my way to the store. On an Electronic marque board at this college *'Your Life Matters'* shone out at me. Those words have been imprinted on my soul ever since. Ten years later, that message is still a part of the messages displayed on that marquee. Over the past year since beginning my podcast "Rediscovering your Passion and Purpose with Patti" part of how I end each episode; I announce 'Life's an Adventure and I want you to Enjoy the Journey because <u>*Your Life Matters*</u>, Thank you and God Bless You All.'

I don't bring up these two stories to be morbid or depressing, I bring them up to remind you that to live your best DASH, you need to really understand and believe that 'your life does matter.' You are a unique and amazing individual that brings great things to our planet. You may not realize the goodness and greatness of your existence, but I am here to tell you right now that your experiences, your triumphs, your struggles all contribute to everything that weaves us together as a species. Your voice deserves to be heard, cherished, and celebrated. Your thoughts, your opinions, your insight, they matter.

They have the power to spark conversations, ignite change, and bridge divides. Your voice is not just an individual sound; it's a ripple that can create waves of transformation. Whether spoken aloud or whispered within, your words have the potential to resonate with someone else's heart, offering solace, encouragement, and hope.

'Never underestimate the impact your voice can have on the lives around you.'

From the moment you took your first breath, you were destined to make an impact. Your presence in this world has the potential to shift the course of history, no matter how small or insignificant your actions may appear. A smile shared with a stranger, a helping hand extended to someone in need, a kind word that uplifts a weary soul, these are all ways we each can make a positive change. Your impact extends far beyond your immediate circle, it has a ripple effect that stretches out into the world, touching lives you may never even be aware of. Humanity is made up of countless individual lives, each interconnected in ways we may never fully comprehend. Your life, your story, your dreams, your voice, are all a part of the great design. You possess the power to inspire, to motivate, and to empower. Your very existence is a testament to resilience and the indomitable human spirit. Through the highs and lows, you have persisted, and that endurance is a beacon of hope for others who may be traveling their own rough paths.

When you look in the mirror, see not just a reflection, but a manifestation of potential. See the culmination of your experiences, your aspirations, and your unique gifts. See someone who is capable of transcending limitations, defying expectations, and embracing the new realms of possibilities. Recognize that you are an author, and every day there is a new page waiting to be written with the ink of your actions and intentions. I want you to embrace your story, for it is a tale of resilience, growth, and determination. Embrace your dreams, they hold the potential to guide you on this journey of life. Embrace your voice, it possesses the power to create meaningful dialogues and create change. Embrace your capacity to impact, to make a difference and show others what it means to be human. When self-doubt begins to creep in, remember this: your life matters and your journey is significant. Your dreams are valid. Your voice is influential. You were born not just to exist, but to thrive and make an impact. As you travel the road of life, may your map guide you towards the things that fill you with passion and purpose. Your story is still being written, and with each mile you travel, you have the power to create a journey that will live on long after you are no longer here. A legacy that boldly declares.

My Life Mattered and I Made a Difference!

Go out there and live your best dash!

Be Daring to Achieve a Successful and Happy life!

CHAPTER TWENTY-SEVEN

BONUS

"It is possible to move a mountain by carrying away the small stones."
Chinese Proverb

Wow! I have come to the final part of my first ever book, time has flown by while writing this book and it just validates for me that I am living my best *Dash* with passion and purpose. I pray that you are as well. Speaking of *"passion and purpose,"* part of that for me is what I learned from someone very dear to me. Her name is Pam Allor. When I was beginning my junior year in college, my advisor needed to take a sabbatical to have her baby. I was very sad that I would have to have a new advisor. That new advisor was Pam. From the moment I first met her to this day forty-three years later, she has not only been my advisor, mentor, colleague, and friend, she is my sister in all ways.

Through the years I have learned so many incredible things from Pam - from teaching and coaching to living life to the fullest. Two of the things that have been a constant learning experience since first meeting Pam has been "happies" and to practice Random Acts of Kindness, She has taught me and demonstrated constantly what it means to live a life with passion and purpose by doing random acts of kindness by having 'happies' ready to give away to people. Sometimes these 'happies' are a piece of candy or a kind word. She carries little happies most of the time. Whether she is giving the cashier a piece of candy and letting them know how much she appreciates them for what they are doing, to complimenting a woman for her beautiful earrings. Pam is an incredible example of practicing random acts of kindness and making people happy, I could go on for many more paragraphs on how Pam has motivated and inspired me, but I want to let you know the new life lessons I have been learning from Pam in the past year and especially over the past couple of months. Five years ago, Pam was involved in a very bad car accident. She sustained injuries to her brain. One of the outcomes from this injury was having memory issues. Through lots of medical tests, a year ago Pam was diagnosed with Lewy body dementia. The comedian Robin Williams was diagnosed with this after he passed away. Lewy body disease affects the central nervous system and autonomic nervous system. Basically, it affects a person mentally and physically.

Over the past year when I have been blessed to be with Pam in person, I see that she is still giving out "happies" and practicing random acts of kindness even though this disease is moving along quickly. Even when mentally, she is not aware of the present moment, she still talks about how important it is to be kind to people and give happies to others. Pam and I have had many incredible conversations, most of which she will not ever remember. On one of my visits, as I was getting ready to leave Pam, she gave me a "happy." It is a beautiful "tree of life" charm and had a wonderful note attached to it. To say this made me 'happy? Yes, it did, I wear it with love, joy, and inspiration.

My point, in all these conversations she spoke about being happy and wanting to write a book about her 'happies.' In this book, she wants to give people examples of the 'happies' she has given away. She wants to explain the meaning of what it really means to practice random acts of kindness and many other things that have to do with being kind. I know that Pam will not be able to write this book. This bonus chapter is Pam's. It includes all the topics and points that Pam has shared with me over the years to this past year and yet to come. 'No one is left' out was a mantra that Pam used from the moment I met her until this very day. She believes it with all her heart and soul. She and Charlene Eichelberger put together a book filled with incredible games and examples of inclusion that they created along with a team of other amazing people, organizations, and I was blessed to be a contributor.

The symbol they chose to use to represent no one is left out was a spiral. Here is what they said about using this symbol; "We decided to use this free form icon as our symbol for inclusion because it represents for us an unending circle that reaches out continually to all the people we teach. We know that our teaching has influenced so many lives and like the spiral, we hope it goes on and on. We don't ever stop. Please join our hands in the circle." Here is their recipe for No One Is Left Out: one part fun, players who support one another, rules that are changed so everyone is included. The game allows players to play with rather than against others, cooperative play, two part 'I can' attitude, one part simple, one part challenging, three parts spirit, and players feel left in.

In a world that seems to be putting self-first no matter what the cost to others, I choose to believe that we are better working together. In the game of life, when we help others up, we lift ourselves in the process. There is too much name calling and putting others down. This following section are parts of lessons Pam taught in my college class I had with her. It is directed at us as future teachers and those already teaching, however, I would like for you to read it just as a human being interacting with others: "Part of a daily lesson plan should be to remind students that there are no put downs allowed in class. Do not ignore racial or homophobic slurs. Teach children what is right and what right looks like in your classroom. Use the Ouch poster, Our Ugly Comments Hurt. We talk about what that means and what as a class we will do to stop the hurt. If someone makes a put-down, the lesson is stopped and the person who made the unacceptable remark owes two put ups to the person they hurt. Please do not be the teacher that contributes to the Conspiracy of Silence. Make your classroom environment a safe, positive, and happy place to learn.

Watch It

Watch your thoughts: They become words.

Watch your words: They become actions.

Watch your actions: They become habits.

Watch your habits: They become your character.

Watch your character: It becomes destiny.

Unknown

Positive Strokes

There are so many ways to help students feel good about themselves: happy messages, happy notes, words of praise, like Let's Cheer for One Another. Examples: The Power Clap, Superpower Clap, Round of Applause, Standing Ovation, A Five Second, Ten Second Stress Reliever, when you feel stressed, irritated or anxious.

1. Smile as you think, my body doesn't need this.

2. Close your eyes, picture yourself in a place you enjoy and breathe deeply three times.

3. As you breathe out, think, I am calm.

4. Open your eyes as you think, I can handle this.

5. Now approach or attack the task or problem.

This is a good technique to use before answering the phone or dealing with a difficult person. Anyone can wait ten seconds.

The Bottom Line

Face it
Nobody owes you a living.
What you achieve or fail to achieve in your lifetime
Is directly related to what you do – or fail to do.
No one chooses his / her parents or childhood,
But you can choose your own direction.
Everyone has problems and obstacles to overcome.
But that, too, is relative to everyone.

Nothing is carved in stone –
You can change anything in your life. If you want
To badly enough.
Excuses are for losers:
Those who take responsibility for their actions.
Are the real winners in life.
Winners meet life's challenges head on knowing there.
Are no guarantees – and give it all they have.
And never think it's too late or too early to begin.
Time plays no favorites and will pass whether.
You act or not.

Take control of your life –
Dare to dream and take risks…
Compete.
If you aren't willing to work for your goals –
Don't expect others to.
Believe in yourself"

HUG POWER

A hug Means –
I share my space with you.
I share my warmth and strength.
And accept yours.
If you ache, I will comfort you.
I do not reject you.
I do not fear you.
Nor will I harm you?
You are not alone.
Somebody cares.
Build a bridge above alienation,
Suspicion, confusion
It has its own language.
And it needs no words.
Changes You and I to We

By Mozzarella

Finally, one of the most recent conversations I had with Pam, during a time of great clarity, I asked her what she wanted me to make sure to put into this bonus chapter to relate to you incredible readers. These are the things she said: 'No one is left out, be loving and accepting, have direction and purpose, apply yourself, establish an environment of inclusion, Practice Random Acts of Kindness every day, it works miracles with every type of learner. I become instead of I can. Having a soft, loving approach to assuring a person they can grow and are important. 'Happies' are hugs of reassurance, happy face on a sign, how powerful that is, and meaningful, it is a validation of that person, makes them feel important, successful, helps people feel like the sky is the limit. Powerful, meaningful pockets full of candies, happy circle, be a slingshot, be a powerful force, be someone's pump for those low moments. When there is no sun, be someone's sunshine.'

After these words of wisdom from Pam, I could begin to see the vail of clarity begin to fade to the background. These words she spoke are imprinted on my heart and soul and have been for the past forty-three years. Pam not only taught them, but she also lives them, she demonstrates in her daily life, all these attributes and more. They are her passion, and her purpose is to share them with as many people as possible, even after she is no longer here. Here legacy is and will continue to make this world a better place to live.

Now that you have come to the end of this book, I pray that part of your passion and purpose is to go out and make someone's day, either by giving them a helping hand, saying an encouraging word, or giving them a physical 'happy.' Not only will you help someone else be happy, but you will also find that you yourself will become happy in the process. What an incredible gift to give to someone else and yourself, go out there and practice random acts of kindness and create a ripple effect that can change our world, it's an amazing way to live your best Dash.

"Carry out a random act of kindness, with no expectation of reward, safe in the knowledge that one day someone might do the same for you."

by Princess Diana

'Here's to living your best Dash.'

Patti

If you enjoyed this book, then my next book

Rediscovering your Passion and Purpose

will be launched 2026.

ABOUT THE AUTHOR

Patti Stueland

Patti Stueland is living her best DASH! Retired after teaching and coaching in public education for "35" years, Patti continues to discover new and exciting adventures. She retired from teaching in June of 2016. July of 2016 is where she began her journey to "Rediscover her Passion and Purpose" for her life. After retirement, Patti began to share her knowledge and experience in various capacities. She became a WASC Evaluator and took on roles as a consultant, creator, and coordinator for the "Cougar Connection", a Freshman Summer Workshop at Granite Hills High School. Additionally, Patti completed her certification from the Celebrant Foundation and Institute, becoming a Life Cycle Celebrant specializing in officiating ceremonies from "Womb to Tomb", with a particular focus on weddings and funerals.

In 2022, Patti began her new adventure as an entrepreneur and began her business "Pathways with Patti". She is a motivational/inspirational speaker, transitional life coach, and podcaster (Rediscovering your Passion and Purpose with Patti) where she talks with people from all over the world who have overcome their life's challenges and obstacles and are helping others to make this world a better place, and she is the contributing author of two #1 Amazon Bestselling books.

As if this wasn't enough, Patti is also an Independent Travel Agent whose business is called "Pathfinder Patti Travel". She takes her passion for travel and helps others to plan and participate in discovering the joys of exploration. Alongside her professional involvement, Patti enjoys pursuing various hobbies and interests, including a passion for woodworking, Zen doodling, and crafting. She refers to herself as a "jack of all trades, master of none.' She also finds joy in traveling, documenting her adventures on social media platforms like Facebook and Instagram. Patti has been traveling the United States full time in her motorhome for the past five years and loves to travel to other countries as well.

Patti's life motto is: 'Make it a great day or not, the choice is yours' and 'Life's an Adventure, Enjoy the Journey.'

Here is to living your best Dash.

If you'd like to connect with Patti.

Pastueland@gmail.com

Pathfinderpattitravel@gmail.com

www.ingramcontent.com/pod-product-compliance
Lightning Source LLC
LaVergne TN
LVHW041220080526
838199LV00082B/1334